TELEPHONE MASTERY
Skills for Business Productivity

by

Mary D. Pekas

PARADIGM

Consulting Editor: **Dr. Rosemary T. Fruehling**
Editorial Director: **Mel Hecker**
Project Editor: **Paul A. Larson**
Writing/Editorial Services: **The Oldham Publishing Service**
Cover Design: **Steve Lundgren**
Illustrations: **Alice Porter**, p. 13
        ©Dynamic Graphics, Inc., pp. 6, 33, 44, 48, 83, 95
        Davis Oldham, pp. 55, 72.

Library of Congress Cataloging–in–Publication Data
Pekas, Mary D.
   Telephone mastery.

   1. Telephone in business. 2. Telephone selling.
I. Title.
HF5541.T4P45 1989   651.7′3   89-10823
ISBN 0-574-20190-4

Printed in the United States of America

10 9 8 7 6 5 4 3

Table of Contents

iv

vii

Telephone Mastery

This course provides a solid foundation for students who want training in the professional use of the telephone. The telephone is our major instrument of communication today in our business and personal lives. We use the telephone to communicate not only over distance, but between offices in the same building and company.

It is a rare business that can operate without the use of a telephone. Not only is the telephone essential for the orderly and successful conduct of most businesses, it is for many the prime method of contact between them and their clients or customers, both actual and prospective. If this telephone contact is pleasant and successful companies prosper. If it is unpleasant and unsuccessful, companies fail.

Because the telephone is such a familiar piece of equipment and in common use in nearly every household as well as every business, the assumption often is made that no special training in its use is required. This assumption is not justified.

Most of you can easily think of a time when you have called a company for service or information, only to be met with indifference, a discourteous tone, a know-nothing, care-less attitude. Or a situation in which the person answering said the company name or department so rapidly and in such a bored monotone, you could not be certain whether you had reached your intended number. And, upon asking for clarification were met with an irritated blare.

Telephone Skills Needed

People in business cannot afford to ignore their telephone skills. A company that spends thousands or millions of dollars in advertising to establish an image would be foolish indeed to ignore the manner in which its people use the telephone. Small companies that do not spend large sums on advertising to create an image must rely not only on the service or product they offer but the image of them created by the people who answer their phones or make their calls.

A successful career in almost any type of business requires telephone skills. Those who master the telephone will increase their value as employees or as potential hires.

Even in the personal use of a telephone at home—for pleasure or business—we can all benefit from improving our telephone techniques.

This course is based on a system of training that was developed during 20 years of professional telephone experience by Mary Pekas, president and founder of Telemarketing Institute, Inc. Clients of Telemarketing Institute include Northwestern Bell, Honeywell, Norwest Banks, Lutheran Brotherhood, General Electric, and Nielsen Market Research.

A Natural Style

Ms. Pekas emphasizes talking on the phone in a natural, friendly manner, as you would face-to-face with a friend. This approach teaches the use of positive voice qualities to project a genuine, service-oriented attitude.

People sometimes feel uneasy using a telephone, partly because of the lack of a visual image. The missing visual image must be replaced by skills that many people have not developed highly—the skill of using one's voice effectively.

Using your voice effectively involves developing a positive attitude as well as selecting the right words. It means articulating the words correctly and clearly, and, in particular, pronouncing the other person's name correctly. It involves projecting interest in your tone and it also involves the important art of listening. Understanding the need to compensate for the missing visual image to inject the human element into telephoning is a first step toward developing professional telephone techniques.

Drawing on her many years of telemarketing experience, the author developed a system that emphasizes the human element. People using this system create a non-pressure, friendly call atmosphere. The style requires integrating the skills of conversation and listening. The course also teaches essential mechanical techniques, such as the necessity of having a neat work area, the need to answer ringing phones promptly, the understanding of telephone numbers, and the use of telephone books to keep costs down.

Whatever business you are in and at whatever level, this course will help you become a more effective user of the telephone. Even if you only use a telephone at home, you will benefit from this course for those times when you make personal business calls—to get information about a product, to check with your city or town hall about a matter significant to you. The telephone is an important tool that you will use often. Learn to use it well.

Performance Skills Checklist

Note that there is a checklist of performance skills in Chapter 9. You can use this in several ways. You can monitor your progress as you study the material in this course. You can keep the list handy as a reminder when you are at work. It could also be interesting to turn to the checklist first and quickly check off the telephone skills you think you have and then compare your skills at the end of the course.

There is also a glossary of special terms. The number appearing in parentheses after each entry is the number of the chapter in which the term first occurs.

xii

Chapter One

Using Telephones in Business

Upon completing this chapter you will be able to:

① *recognize telephone benefits and drawbacks,*

② *identify three factors on which professional telephone skills depend,*

③ *recognize that appropriate telephone skills are applied in different situations,*

④ *identify three reasons why professional telephone skills are important.*

Of all communication devices, telephones are still the most often used in the modern business office, the first things to be installed after the electricity and plumbing. This is true even though many other ways to communicate over telephone wires exist—*fax (facsimile) machines, modems, telexes*. For many people and businesses, telephones long ago replaced the written note or letter for communicating over short as well as great distances. Whether you are at work or at home, telephones play a role in your life. Knowing how to use them effectively is important.

Despite the fact that telephones are everywhere and we all use them, not every one uses them well. People have strong feelings about the phone. Some people hate them, finding them intrusive and impersonal. Others feel lost without their telephone link to the world. Some people are uncomfortable on the phone. They miss the visual contact. They want to see the person with whom they are talking.

Some people are naturals using the phone. If you were to watch and listen to them talking on the phone, you might be able to analyze what they do and learn ways of working with the phone. This book will help you analyze what makes an effective telephone user and sharpen your telephone skills.

Whenever you use a phone, either at home or at work, you want to project an agreeable telephone personality. At work it is important because when you use the phone on your job, you are not only speaking for yourself; you are representing the company. The image you project is the company's image to the person on the other end of the line. If you project a negative image, the person may decide not to continue doing business with your company.

Recognizing Telephone Benefits and Drawbacks

Many people have mixed feelings about the telephone, even though it provides many benefits, such as being able to dial a number and get information on anything from what is showing at the movies to whether a store has a product you want. Following the phone company's slogan,

"Let your fingers do the walking..." can save you a great deal of time and frustration.

Other benefits include allowing you to socialize at a moment's notice with friends and keep in touch with family. If you need information at work, you can call a coworker or client. You can take an order or give someone directions. It is the best and quickest way to reach an emergency service, such as an ambulance or fire company. It is a wonderful tool, and seems to be indispensable for modern life.

However, the phone has its drawbacks as well. We have all had the experience, at home and at work, of feeling exasperated at times at the interruptions the phone brings into our lives. We are able to do with a phone what we would never do in person: open the door of a house or office, walk right in, and ask to be spoken to regardless of what the other person is doing. Because of this, it is important to learn how to place and receive calls to minimize the annoyance and enhance the benefits of business telephone use.

Another drawback is that the phone does not produce a written record to refer back to after the conversation is over. Effective phone use therefore involves knowing how to take written messages, notes, and other important information.

Most businesses have procedures that specify how certain tasks are to be accomplished. Part of your job training will include learning your company's procedures for the telephone, which will help you to realize the benefits and deal with the drawbacks of phone use.

Defining Professional Telephone Skills

Any time you pick up the telephone receiver and dial a number, you begin a series of activities that can be considered telephone skills. In general, the skills you use during a call depend on three factors:

✓ the telephone equipment,

✓ the kind of call you are placing or receiving,

✓ your personal attributes—voice, knowledge, and attitude.

Telephone Skills and Equipment

Some telephone skills are mechanical. You will need mechanical skills simply to use correctly the particular kind of phone equipment you have. Along with some of these pieces of equipment come special dialing requirements for inside phones and extensions; for placing direct long distance calls or local outside calls. It is important to become familiar with 800 numbers, area codes, and time zones.

When you first take a job, part of your orientation to the company will be learning the mechanics of using the phone system. You will probably learn these telephone skills quickly and easily. If your company has a cumbersome system that makes it difficult for you to transfer inbound calls, or you spend a lot of time on the phone without an appropriate headset, you may have to develop telephone techniques to overcome these difficulties.

4

Telephone Skills and Various Kinds of Calls

Selling, receiving or making complaints, arranging appointments, sending or receiving information, and just being friendly are all tasks accomplished via a phone call. Each task requires a different approach or skill. For example, selling requires you to be well-informed about a certain line of products, to be persuasive, and to place many follow-up phone calls. Handling a complaint requires you to develop assertiveness, patience, and diplomacy.

You will read of many of the different kinds of calls you may have to handle in business. Each has its own techniques for placing or answering, concluding and closing. You may be required to learn how to get past a protective secretary or you may be a protective secretary.

Many companies have definite procedures to follow for different phone situations. The most common is the greeting. Each company wants its name mentioned, and many require that the person answering the phone give his or her name: "Good morning, this is Acme Tools, Bill Jordan speaking."

There may be procedures for handling certain types of calls. Calls for information are handled one way; complaint calls are handled another way. The company may prefer certain people to be spokespersons: "Ms. Brown handles these questions. Would you please *hold* while I *transfer* your call?"

Your Personal Telephone Skills

Because it is true that anyone who answers the phone *is* the company to the caller, what you know and how you express yourself becomes a reflection of your firm. Your voice is the only impression callers receive of you—and of the company. You already have a telephone personality. Whenever you use the phone, your manner, voice, and techniques reflect your personality. For informal, every-day use of the phone between friends, your personal telephone style is probably adequate. In the business world, and for some personal business calls, you may find that you need to develop other techniques.

Your personal telephone skills depend on your knowledge and experience, how much you know about your company's business, the grammar you use. Your telephone manner will be affected by how you use your voice and body, the tone of your voice, and your attitude toward the person who called or is being called.

Many of us take our voices for granted and never consider how they might sound to another, especially when transmitted electronically. You have no doubt seen the comic characterization of the whiny, nasal-voiced operator who exaggerates pronunciation. It is funny until that grating voice comes flying over the wire into your ear.

5

Vocal habits such as inflection, pronunciation, the pauses you use all affect your telephone techniques. How you sit, breathe, and even the expression on your face affect how your voice sounds over the phone. Your voice reveals your moods and attitudes—sometimes without your realizing it. When you are annoyed at the phone ringing, it is all too easy to sound abrupt and irritated when you answer. On the other hand, exaggerated and insincere friendliness is as noticeable and will block communication as much as an unpleasant approach.

Becoming aware of how your voice represents your attitudes is the first step to learning how to manage your verbal expression for more successful telephone techniques.

Applying Telephone Skills

Everyone working in a business needs to know how to use the phone effectively, no matter what the nature of the business is, what size it is, or where it is located. The telephone is an important tool to communicate to others within one company and outside. Different situations require phone skills appropriate to each situation.

Business is Conducted Over the Phone

Obvious situations where the telephone is used include the receptionists' desk, and the customer service department. Here is a short list of other places where people use the phone to conduct business.

✓ The sales person in a store handles calls from customers who want to know if the store carries certain items.

✓ The auto mechanic handles calls from prospects who ask questions about their car and arranges appointments for services.

✓ The clerk in a small shop, such as a plumber's, handles calls to arrange appointments for work to be done.

✓ The secretary in a multimillion dollar company handles calls from executives within the company seeking information about work done in the department.

✓ The school teacher talks to parents about the students' work.

✓ The travel agent makes reservations over the phone.

✓ The hostess in a restaurant takes reservations, tells what credit cards are accepted, if there is a dress requirement.

6

All these people are more successful in their work when they deal with people effectively, helpfully, and courteously on the phone.

Different Techniques for Different Companies

You will use different telephone techniques depending on the size and nature of your company and your job. Employees with companies whose business comes mostly by telephone have the most obvious need for professional telephone skills. These companies are more likely to provide training in phone use and require the use of logs, call reports, and other forms for recording information.

Large companies have different needs from small companies, requiring slight variations in the techniques used. The differences may begin the moment a call is received. Large companies may be structured so that the first person a caller speaks to is a switchboard operator. In a small business it may be a receptionist or even the owner.

Different phone techniques may be required depending on the degree of specialization in the work done by employees. In a large company some employees may never communicate with clients and customers, while others may only handle a specific type of call, such as taking orders or dealing with the media.

The kinds of telephoning outside the company that each worker does will be different from one another. For each individual, however, one call may not be very different from another. The professional tele-

Each company will have its own procedures for making and receiving telephone calls.

phone skills each uses may be essentially the same all day.

On the other hand, in some small businesses, everyone must be able to handle all kinds of call. A worker in this situation must be flexible and use many kinds of telephone techniques in the course of a day.

Differences between large and small companies also are reflected in the degree of formality with which customers and business callers are treated. Generally, a large company will be more formal in addressing callers, while in a small company many customers are on a first-name basis.

High Stress Situations

From time to time almost anyone in any business can experience a high stress situation on the phone. Some people will be in situations daily that are stressful. Sometimes, the stress has a positive effect, sometimes a negative one.

Telemarketing—the use of the telephone to generate revenue by making sales, handling orders, providing customer service, or arranging appointments for selling—can be stressful at times as well as rewarding. It requires you to be quick, attentive, and responsive. Doing this kind of activity with a high level of energy throughout the day takes special telephone techniques. Difficult or awkward situations are stressful. Collection agencies and complaint departments can mean high stress work. Agencies that provide a service to people in times of trouble—insurance offices, lawyers, or social services—are environments with potentially stressful phone calls.

Not everyone communicates well under stress. It is a skill, however, that can be learned and one that, with practice, becomes almost second nature. Telephone skills designed to defuse difficult situations or to clarify confusing messages can reduce the stress level both for the caller and the person who answers the phone. You will learn how to recognize a potentially tense situation before it develops into something that cannot be easily managed. You will learn techniques to use to turn potentially tense situations into positive and productive experiences.

There are communication methods that create opportunities for receiving and sending clear messages, for restating messages to be sure both people have the same understanding of the message. These techniques will be explored in this text, and you will learn how to apply them to your work on the telephone.

Recognizing Importance of Telephone Skills

If you have a job that requires you to answer the phone frequently, it is easy to slip into bad habits, such as answering in a tone of voice that tells the caller you are uninterested. Or, you may overdo trying to sound friendly. Acquiring professional skills for telephoning will help you avoid these pitfalls.

You Are the Company

For many businesses, the telephone is a major link with the world. It is often the only contact many customers have with them. You will find that you communicate with some people regularly by phone although you never meet face to face. The only impression they have of you and your company is what they receive over the phone.

When the telephone is the major—or only—way you have to communicate with others, your voice is the only impression they receive of you and of the company. This impression is intensified because the sound of the other person's voice is closer and more immediate on the phone than it is in person.

Listeners focus on the sound because they are not receiving *visual* or *tactile* information. **Visual** refers to what is seen. **Tactile** refers to what is felt. If the speaker's voice does not have a helpful sound, we cannot look at his or her face to evaluate that impression.

The Phone As a Sales Tool

All companies have something to sell—if not products, then services. Much care is put into presenting that product or service to the public. Even if you never have an opportunity to sell the product or service over the phone, each time you lift the receiver you have the opportunity to sell the company—to express the company's goodwill to its customers and clients.

The unconscious misuse of the telephone can do much to undermine all the careful effort to present products and services favorably. It can become a weak link in the company's communication with the world. Profits and growth are at risk.

It is important to understand both the obvious sales function of the phone and the not-so-obvious sales-enhancing use of the phone. As you learn telephone techniques, you will become aware of how you can more effectively contribute to your company's profitability merely by being more skilled at using the phone.

Improving Skills Enhances Work Satisfaction

Do you remember the first time you learned to do something—ride a bike, play tennis? You may have found it difficult and frustrating at first—fallen off your bike, missed the serves. You may have wondered why you ever wanted to do this, decided it was no fun, and that you were not going to do it any longer. If you stuck it out, you may have added a new and enjoyable activity to your life.

Acquiring certain office skills may have a lot in common with your early experiences with bike riding or tennis playing. As you progress through this book, try to be aware of your own abilities and needs, and give the ideas and suggestions a try. Some of the ideas may not work for you. Others may change your daily experience with the phone. As with any skill, the more able you become, the more enjoyment you will experience. Your job satisfaction improves and you become a more valuable employee.

9

Quiz Questions

1. Name some benefits and drawbacks of the telephone and explain the importance of professional telephone skills.

2. What three factors determine the telephone skills to use?

3. Give at least two examples of purely mechanical telephone techniques.

4. You read that "Many companies have definite procedures to follow for different phone situations." Give an example of a common procedure and at least one other time when procedures used require professional telephone skills.

5. Underline the correct choices. Telephone skills affected by your personality can include your knowledge and experience; your understanding of grammar; supervisor's attitude; tone of voice; attitude toward the person who called or is being called; product lines; inflection; customer's knowledge; distinctness of pronunciation; facial expression.

6. List five different business situations that require phone skills and explain how the phone is used in each.

7. Give two examples of stressful telephone situations.

8. Why is it important to remember, when on the company phone, that you are the company?

9. Name two benefits you receive when you improve your telephone skills.

Discussion Questions

1. Discuss some of the many new sophisticated ways to communicate—modems, telexes, and fax (facsimile) machines—and why the telephone is still important.

2. What is meant by your personal telephone style? Discuss how your style is developed.

3. Discuss why almost everyone in business needs to know how to use the phone effectively. Give some specific examples of how people use the phone to conduct business.

4. Discuss some of the differences that large and small companies may have in telephone skills their employees use.

Activities

1. This activity is to increase your awareness of how the telephone affects both caller and receiver. Write down what you can remember of at least two business calls (to place a catalog order, arrange an appointment, to seek information). Now analyze what happened in the conversation. Write what you liked or did not like about the exchange; what you would copy or what you would do differently if you were the one on the other end.

2. Now is a good time to think about what your strengths and weaknesses are in using the phone. Make a list of each. Consider the things you like best about calling, and the phone calls you always put off. Try to remember what happens while you are talking on the phone; does the other person frequently say, "I'm sorry, could you repeat that?" Do you have difficulty terminating a call? Do you get tongue-tied when talking with a stranger? List as many things as you can. Keep these lists to refer to later.

Chapter Two

Developing Efficient Telephone Use

Upon completing this chapter you will be able to:

① *identify modern telephone equipment,*

② *analyze a typical phone number,*

③ *use five techniques for keeping an organized workstation,*

④ *recognize and use all features of a typical telephone directory.*

I n this chapter you will learn about different kinds of telephone equipment and how to place calls—both routine and special. Developing professional telephone techniques begins with a comfortable familiarity with the equipment, a well set-up work station, and your knowledge and confidence in placing calls.

Knowing Your Telephone Equipment

Telephone equipment includes everything from the phone book to the rotary dial telephone to sophisticated programmable phones. This section describes some of the equipment you are likely to encounter in the modern office.

Basic Telephone Equipment

Although equipment is changing, two basic types of telephones are in general use. One is the **rotary dial phone** and the other is the **push button phone**, which is also known as a **Touch-tone phone**.

Many offices have phones that perform more than just the basic function of dialing numbers. If your office has one of these phones, be sure to study the manual that explains how to use it.

The rotary phone has the circular disk with holes in it. Each hole opens on a number—from 0 to 9—and, except at the one and zero holes, three letters. All letters of the alphabet except "Q" and "Z" are represented. When you dial a number, the disk makes a clicking sound audible in the room as it moves back to its starting position.

Touch-tone phones are "dialed" by pressing numbers. They make no sound audible in the room. But they make different toned beeps in the receiver for each number pressed, hence the name "Touch-tone." These phones have four rows of three buttons each. Ten of the 12 buttons have a number from 0 to 9 and letters in the same arrangement as the dial phones. The zero is the middle button on the bottom row. The left button is an asterisk or star (*) and the right button is a pound or number symbol (#).

It takes less time to use a push button phone, and they may replace rotary phones altogether some day.

In time, you may be able to do many financial transactions by using Touch-tone phones. The additional keys with the asterisk and number symbols are used now by many companies that have 800 numbers and automatic answering devices. You are asked to push the asterisk or number symbol to choose among alternatives given you.

Extensions and Transfers

In some offices, a desk telephone may have two or more **extension** lines that can be answered. Usually, in addition to those used for dialing, there are buttons for each extension which flash when the number rings. You press it to answer the call.

Each button has an assigned *extension number*. An **extension number** is the additional number—usually three digits, but it can be two or four—for individual phones within a company. For example, the number 111-2222x333 indicates that the main company number is 111-2222 and this particular individual phone has the extension 333.

In addition to the buttons for the extensions there is also a **hold button**. This allows the person answering a call to put it on hold if another call comes in on another extension. If the call is to be transferred, it is put on hold while the **transfer** is made.

Phones with the capability of taking calls for many other phones are known as **call directories**. They are small **switchboards**. If the line is not busy, the call is transferred by pushing the button with the extension's number.

Telephone Accessories

In offices where phone work is constant, **headsets** may be provided. A headset combines a receiver and microphone in a unit worn on the head or under the chin. It leaves your hands free to write or use a keyboard or take notes, and is more comfortable for constant use than a standard phone receiver. Headsets are often used by switchboard operators and in telemarketing.

Sometimes **shoulder rests** are attached to office telephones,

A typical modern office phone has several extensions, each with its own number.

13

14

enabling you to tuck the receiver between shoulder and ear, leaving hands free. However, shoulder and neck muscles can become cramped using them. Also, you may be unable to move your jaw freely, making it hard to speak clearly. They also restrict the air from your lungs and the movement of your vocal cords, which affects fluency and delivery.

Specialized Telephone Equipment

More sophisticated telephones enable businesses to meet special needs and you will probably encounter examples of these telephones in your business career. An executive may have a **programmable phone** with frequently dialed numbers stored in its **memory**. Each number can be dialed by pressing one button. These phones have a separate set of buttons reserved for this purpose. Numbers are assigned to the buttons by the user.

A **speaker phone** makes it possible for several people to participate in a telephone conversation. The phone has a microphone that is capable of picking up voices at a distance and its speaker can broadcast loudly enough to be heard by a room full of people. This is not the same as a *conference call*, which you read about later.

Automatic redial is a feature many phones have. The phone can be programmed to remember a number and can be set to dial it continuously until the call can be completed. Reaching constantly busy numbers can take a lot of time if you have to redial the number manually. Automatic redialing saves that effort.

Computerized Touch-tone phones are used in many offices today. These are regular Touch-tone phones that are connected to com-

The rotary phone gave us the expression "to dial a number." We still talk of "dialing" even when we use a push button phone. If you look in a telephone directory, you will see the verb "dial" used often.

Because we are used to the expression "dial a number," it sounds slightly odd to talk of "pushing" or "pressing" a number. However, you will hear this expression if you call a company with an automated answering system. You will be told that if you have a Touch-tone phone, to press numbers according to your needs.

You might get a message such as "If you are using a Touch-tone phone, press 1 for billing information, press 2 to place an order. Make your selection now."

puter programs that allow the user to do such things as record, screen, date, and relay messages. Companies with such systems have manuals explaining their operation. A user can also get a voice recording of tips or help by pushing one of the buttons, usually the # button. A typical manual would tell you what buttons to push for different activities. These lists are called **menus** and one might have these items with the number being the button you push:

1. Listen to new messages.
2. Record and send a message.
3. Enter phone manager.
5. Listen to previously saved messages.
0 Transfer to operator.
* Exit this session.
# Get help.

15

After making a selection, you may have further choices. For example, if you push 3 for phone manager, you then have several choices for changing message, setting security code, recording a personal greeting, and so forth.

Anatomy of a Telephone Number

Telephone numbers are made up of three parts: the *area code*, the *exchange* number and the specific, local number assigned to an individual, house, or company.

Local numbers consist of the familiar seven digits. The first three are the *exchange numbers*. The **exchange numbers** identify a specific geographic area. Very small towns might have one exchange but most communities have several exchanges based on neighborhoods. Your **local area**, the telephone area in which you need dial only the local number, will usually have several exchanges in it. The last four digits are the numbers of a specific person or business.

For telephoning purposes, the country (the whole world, for that matter) is divided into areas, each of which is assigned an **area code**. Smaller or less populous states have just one area code. Connecticut, for example, is 203; Utah is 801. Large, heavily populated states have two or more area codes. California has 10, Texas 7, and New York 8.

When you dial outside your area code you need to dial a one first: 1 + area code + the seven digit number. If you dial outside your local area but within your area code, you need only add the one: 1 + the seven digit number. Depending on the phone company being used, the procedure may vary slightly. But the area code and local number combination is standard.

Using your knowledge of how telephone numbers are made up helps you handle calls quickly and efficiently. For example, if you get a message with just the area code and number, you can tell where it is from and decide the best time to call back. Knowing the exchange tells you whether you need to dial a 1 first or if it is a local call.

Organizing Your Workstation

Unless you will have to spend an extraordinary amount of time on the phone, your workstation will not have to be adjusted for easy phone use. Obviously, you want your phone to be located where you can reach it without having to move from the desk. It should be on the same side of the desk as the hand you use to pick up the receiver. Aside from those considerations, the only other arrangements you have to make for professional telephone techniques are the same that enable you to do your desk work professionally.

A Neat and Organized Desk

Imagine you have called your accountant's office to ask a question about this year's income tax. The receptionist answers professionally and puts you right through to your accountant's assistant, who takes your name and says, "One moment, please, while I locate your file." What you hear then is the opening and closing of drawers, shuffling papers, then someone muffles the phone, and says, "George, have you seen that file for the Martins?" You hear more scrambling around. You wait patiently. At last, "Oh, yes, here is your file. Can you wait another second while I find my pencil?"

You would probably be losing confidence in your accountant by now. A neat workstation is necessary to use telephones professionally. Here are a few suggestions for keeping your work area neat:

✓ Avoid having piles of papers on your desk—messages and information can get buried. Use clearly labeled files, which can be kept in vertical holders on your desk if needed constantly.

✓ Have a wall or desk calendar on which to record appointments, deadlines, assignments. Maintain a "to be done" file.

✓ Make notes on file-sized paper—not scraps, which can get lost. If you receive a call about a memo you sent, put the message on a copy of the memo so that all the information is in one place.

✓ If you do jot information on a scrap of paper, take time to transfer it to a larger piece that you can file appropriately.

✓ Keep only what you need on your desk to perform your duties and to respond to calls promptly and professionally.

Tools for Taking Messages

Taking messages and getting them to the right person is an important part of telephone skills. To do this well, you should:

✓ Keep pens and pencils in reach. If people have a habit of "borrowing" them, keep a secret supply in another drawer.

✓ Keep a supply of message pads, order blanks, scrap paper (adhesive backed notes are very useful)—whatever your job requires—near the phone. Specially designed "while you were out" message pads are available that provide spaces for everything you need to record to take an effective message.

✓ Leave messages where people will be able to spot them easily. That means not leaving them on a desk cluttered with other paper. A good idea is to leave the message on a person's chair, either resting on the seat or taped to the back.

Tools for Placing Calls

You can waste a lot of time looking for a phone number. Besides your phone directory, you may wish to have, on hand, some of the following:

✓ in a large organization, a company directory containing numbers and extension numbers;

✓ a short list of your most frequently called in-house extensions or outside phone numbers posted on the wall near your phone, or taped to your desktop;

✓ a rotating or flip-through index file with removeable cards on which you can put any numbers (and mailing addresses) you think you will use again.

Using the Telephone Directory

A much neglected piece of telephone equipment is the **telephone directory**—the **phone book**. Made available free by the telephone company to anyone who has a telephone, the phone book is a treasure house of information.

17

Getting Acquainted with Your Telephone Directory

Nearly all phone books have *white pages* and *yellow pages*. The **yellow pages** are familiar to us as the section with advertisements and listings for businesses and services. These pages are sometimes indexed on pages of still another color—green, for example. The **white pages** consist of general information and the lists of phone numbers.

18

What do phone books offer the user? A great deal. Because the telephone company is now no longer one nationwide monopoly, but rather consists of many smaller regional companies, there is quite a bit of variety in what phone directories will offer from region to region. Here is a sample of what you might find in a phone book:

- © an easy-to-locate place where you can write emergency numbers for fire, police, and ambulance

- © statewide zip codes

- © toll-free poison information hotline

- © phone numbers for State Police, FBI, Secret Service

- © community service telephone numbers or "Helplines" for information about everything from child abuse to legal services to volunteer services

- © maps of areas covered by the phone book

- © telephone customer rights and responsibilities

- © safety and protection information

- © complete instructions for placing any kind of call

- © complete information on doing business with the telephone company, from installation and repair to types of service available to billing and payment

- © an area code and time zone map

- © area codes for large cities in the United States

- © international codes for many countries and cities

- © street addresses for most listings

- © information on how to save money on phone calls

In densely populated areas, there may be blue pages and gold pages as well. Blue pages contain numbers for government—federal, state and municipal—offices and departments. Gold pages contain a senior citizen's guide to discounts and services, often in a large print.

In front of the white pages there are usually several pages on the basics of phone use: how to do business with the phone company, how to place calls, and how to use the directory including **directory assistance**, which most of us call *information*. It helps you get numbers not listed in the book. Try always to have an up-to-date directory.

Finding Numbers in the Telephone Directory

Phone numbers are organized by community. Sometimes small towns are grouped together. If you cannot find a town, check the front of the phone book for a list and instructions for finding entries. Telephone books list entries alphabetically by last names of individuals and first major word in company names (not including "the" and "a"). They list names by letter order: "MacDonald" and "Maz..." come before McDonald. Names with initials—"L G Marine"—precede names that have initials with "and"—"L and G Builders"—and these precede names that start with "La...." Abbreviations and numbers are listed as if spelled out.

Using Directory Assistance

If you cannot find the number you want in the phone book, use directory assistance, or information. Check the directory's front pages for the number to call for information within your area code, as it may vary. It is usually 411. For numbers in other area codes—long-distance numbers—the number to dial is 1 + Area Code + 555-1212.

Nearly all directory information is computerized. Often the assisting operator is located far from the place you are trying to reach. Have accurate spelling for names, and accurate addresses to help the operator locate the number. Directory assistance calls cost money. Some phone companies allow a limited number of such calls within the area code and charge for calls over that limit. Most charge for out-of-state assistance calls. Write numbers down to reduce costly directory assistance calls.

Money Saving Ideas

Everyone likes to save money on telephone calls, especially costly long distance calls. In the front of many phone directories is a page of cost-cutting measures. Here are a few ideas:

✓ Before placing long distance calls, plan what you want to say and write it down.

✓ Call during bargain hours as much as you can.

✓ Dial direct whenever possible.

✓ Take advantage of toll-free "800" numbers.

Quiz Questions

20

1. Describe the two basic types of phones used today.

2. What are three disadvantages to holding the phone with your shoulder?

3. Name four types of specialized telephone equipment.

4. Name the three parts of a typical telephone number.

5. Describe what you can find in the white, yellow, and blue pages of a telephone directory.

6. List three tools for telephone message taking and three tools for placing telephone calls.

7. How are phone numbers organized and listed in the telephone directory?

8. List two ideas to lower phone bills.

Discussion Questions

1. Discuss with classmates the kinds of phone equipment they have had experience with including the equipment mentioned in the text and any not mentioned.

2. Explain how to create a neat workstation. Discuss the value of having a work area organized in regard to professional telephone techniques.

Activities

1. Get acquainted with your phone book. Look up and write down all you can learn about services for the disabled, consumer law, direct dialing.

Chapter Three

Managing Business Telephone Calls

Upon completing this chapter you will be able to:

① *use four skills for all calls,*

② *use three guidelines for ending calls,*

③ *handle inbound calls with professional skills,*

④ *place outbound calls with professional skills,*

⑤ *use answering machines as a positive tool.*

In this chapter you will read about the telephone skills that will help you project a courteous, helpful, professional attitude. You will identify general telephone skills needed in all calls, as well as specific techniques for answering inbound calls and placing outbound calls that will make your use of the phone effective and professional. You will also learn skills for special calls.

In large companies, it may not be possible for you to dial outside or receive calls from outside the company directly. In such a situation, your inbound calls will be forwarded to you by the switchboard operator, and you go through the switchboard to place outside calls.

Some companies equip their phone systems with an **access number** (often 9), which you dial to use an outside line. You then can dial local and, depending on company policy, long distance numbers. Some companies restrict long distance dialing. In such cases, unauthorized employees would not be able to dial long distance because the access number would open up only local lines. Other companies might require all long distance calls to go through the switchboard.

Some companies give their executives special access lines so that they can place long distance calls directly or personal calls charged to phone company charge cards. Some require employees to keep a log of all long distance calls and the purpose of each. The reason for these procedures is to keep down telephone costs, which could soar if hundreds of people were making frequent long distance calls.

Calls fall into two general categories—*direct* and *operator assisted*. **Direct** calls are calls you complete yourself. **Operator assisted** calls are those requiring you to dial the operator to make the call. These include collect, person-to-person, bill to third party, mobile land, air and marine, conference, and international calls.

Developing Skills for All Calls

As you read in Chapter One, when you use the phone, your voice is the only way others have to form an impression of you and your company. In Chapter Seven you will learn how to project a positive image over the phone. The professional telephone skills you learn in this chapter contain the basic elements of positive helpfulness and are the key to creating a professional impression on the phone.

Identify Yourself Immediately

Identify yourself and your company as soon as the person you call picks up the phone or as soon as you answer a call. It is probably instinctive with you to introduce yourself when you meet someone face to face. Perhaps, when you are on the phone, not being able to see the other person keeps that instinct from taking over. But it is precisely because people cannot see each other on the phone that it is even more important to identify yourself.

23

Even if you think that someone should recognize your voice, do not assume that. Perhaps you have received a call in which an unidentified caller began a friendly, informal conversation, confident that you would recognize whose voice it was. You may have had a moment of embarrassed confusion as you searched your memory or waited for some clue in the conversation for an identification. Socially this is a rude thing to do; in business, it is rude and unprofessional.

First Name vs. Last Name

A cartoon in a national magazine shows a couple sitting at a restaurant table with a waiter by their side, who has just said: "Hello, my name is Michael and I am your waiter tonight." One of the diners responds, "Do you mind if I call you waiter, Michael?"

There is a tendency toward the use of first names in many situations which, as the cartoon suggests, not everyone enjoys. First names are used more frequently in some parts of the country than in others. Some businesses have an informal atmosphere that encourages first name use. Some have a formal atmosphere that discourages it. Some people like be called by their first names and call others by theirs. Some dislike strangers using their first name.

The best thing to do is to ask courteously what the person prefers, by saying, "Do you prefer that I call you by your first or last name?" Or, "Do you prefer to be called by your first or last name?"

Whether *you* give just your first name or your full name, when placing or receiving calls, will depend on company policy, the image you want to project, and how you feel about others using your name. These will also affect whether you use a title, such as Mr., Miss, Doctor, Ms., Professor, or Mrs. Although providing your full name—first and last—does project a more formal image than using a first name only, it is much harder for the caller to remember.

Whether you call others by their first or last names will depend on company policy, how well you know them, and their personal preferences. Some business organizations may prefer you to use a person's title to maintain formality. Sometimes titles are used when addressing individuals in recognition of their position or age. You may find yourself naturally addressing older people or people in supervisory positions by title and last name, and it is a good policy to do so until they ask you to call them by their first names. The best way is simply to ask the person how he or she would prefer to be addressed.

24   *Write Down Correct Spelling and Pronunciations*

With all telephone calls, write down the other person's name immediately; if necessary, ask your caller to repeat the name—do not hesitate to ask for a spelling and/or a correct pronunciation. People appreciate your caring enough to have the spelling and pronunciation accurate. This simple act will save you the embarrassment of having to ask for the name again later, or worse, not be able to do follow-up work because you cannot remember a name.

One hint on pronouncing a name correctly: ask for the spelling and pronunciation, and write it down **phonetically**—that is, how it sounds—repeat it back to them. People appreciate your carefulness, and certainly prefer to be asked than to be mispronounced.

At any point in a conversation, you may realize that you will need to return the call—for example, after you have had time to get more information, or because you have to leave for an appointment and cannot

---

What if you do not know someone's title? There may be times when you not only do not know a title, you do not even know a first or last name.

For example, you may return to your desk to find a message: "L. Johnson called—please call back at 334-6720." If you do not know L. Johnson and no one is around to tell you whether it was a man or woman who called, then try this strategy.

Return the call and say, "Hello, this is (your name). I'm returning a call to an L. Johnson. Could you assist me with this person's complete name and title?"

Whether a secretary or "L. Johnson" answers the phone, you will find out the person's name, as both of them will be very open to assisting you with this information.

finish the discussion. Before you end the call, ask for and agree on a good time to call back. Then, to maintain your professional image, make sure you call back at the agreed upon time.

Ending Calls Gracefully

There are professional telephone skills for ending all calls gracefully. Generally, whoever places the call ends it.

25

> ✓ *If you are the caller*: Once you have finished your business, which you want to keep as brief as possible, you can say, "Thanks for your time and attention. Good-bye, (name)." Wait for the other person to respond before replacing the receiver. Or you can say, "I certainly appreciate the time you took to go over things with me. Do you have anything else you'd like to cover?" Be sensitive to the other person's wishes on closing the conversation.

> ✓ *If you have received the call*: You can expect the caller to end the conversation. There are some graceful ways, however, for you to initiate the closing. For example, you can say, "Thanks very much for your call," or, "It was certainly good to hear from you. Please call again whenever you need assistance." Or you can tell the caller, in summing up the conversation, what your next course of action will be: "I will let you know right away when I have...." Let the caller hang up first.

> ✓ *If you are trapped by a talkative caller*: One of the most challenging situations is receiving a call from a very talkative person. In business, a great deal of time can be lost unless workers who use the phone know how to end such calls courteously. The best way is to be as polite as you can (even though the talkative one is not being polite) but be *absolutely clear*: "I'm sorry to interrupt; however, I have a call holding on the other line. We thank you for your call and certainly hope I have satisfied your concerns for now."

Developing Skills for Inbound Calls

In business, the inbound call is both an opportunity and an interruption. Unless your job is answering the phone, calls are sure to come when you are doing an important task you must finish. Nevertheless, inbound calls mean new customers or old customers calling for services or products. All calls deserve your professional telephone skills.

Watch Your Attitude

A ringing phone can stimulate a surge of irritation at the interruption, if the person is in the middle of a project, or a bored reaction at having to answer the phone yet one more time. An irritated person may answer so abruptly as to seem rude, or mumble so rapidly as to be unintelligible. When the telephone rings, professionals handle all calls with a positive, can-do attitude. They quickly suppress feelings of irritation or boredom so that their voices are clear and express a service-oriented attitude.

26

Answer Promptly

People are accustomed to expect that a business call will be answered within the first three rings. Always try to answer within five rings. Five rings takes about 30 seconds, which seems a short time—unless you happen to be the one calling and waiting for someone to answer.

If someone does not answer a home phone promptly, people are not annoyed. No one expects people at home to be sitting by the phone. If a business phone is not answered promptly, however, we are critical. Businesses have phones to conduct business. If business people do not answer their phones promptly, we logically conclude they are not particularly interested in our business.

Identify Yourself Clearly

You will read often that you are to identify yourself immediately upon placing a call or handling an inbound call. But there is more: In a business setting you are to identify yourself and your company or department _clearly_. Everyone answering a business phone immediately gives his or her name and the company name. Sometimes endless repetition causes people to mumble or slur over the names so quickly that the caller cannot be sure of having reached the right company. So, identify yourself immediately—clearly.

Most companies have a preferred greeting that you will use. For example: "Good morning, this is the Bennett Group, Marjorie Brown speaking." Or, "Thank you for calling Trevelyn's Ltd. This is Joan. May I help you?"

In larger companies, when you are answering a department or division phone, remember that the caller may have been shunted around from other departments before reaching you. Your promptness and professionalism will defuse any annoyance the caller may feel. Answer the phone with the department name and your own name.

Atty. Browning was due back in the courtroom where his case was taking longer than he expected. He needed to call his office and quickly leave a message that he would not be returning until later in the day, and that his assistant should cancel his afternoon appointments.

When the receptionist answered the phone, all Browning heard was "Please, hold—*click*!" To his exasperation, he was put on hold much longer than he could comfortably wait.

Understandably, he was furious by the time the receptionist put him through. And he could not help wondering what it must be like for clients to call his office.

If you are picking up other people's lines, identify whose phone it is as completely as you can; for example, "Accounting, Leslie Green's desk, Nancy Curtis speaking."

Transfer and Hold

As with answering the phone, your company may have procedures for *transferring* or putting calls on *hold*. When a call is on hold, the caller hears nothing and it seems as if the phone line were dead. Or they may hear music or a radio station, which some people find annoying. Inform callers about what you will be doing and why. For example, you could say "I think customer service can best answer your question. Let me transfer you to Owen Morris. Please hold on." If the person is on hold more than 30 seconds, you should check to see if they wish to keep waiting.

Be sensitive to long distance calls. Ask permission before transferring or holding these calls. Say, for example, "It will be a moment before Mrs. Greene can take your call. Would you like to hold or shall I ask her to return your call?" Give the caller the choice. Never put callers on hold without asking whether they wish it. A growing practice is for someone to answer the phone, identify the company, and say, "I must put you on hold, please wait." Then, without waiting for a response, put the caller on hold. This antagonizes people.

There is also a courteous way to talk to the person in the company to whom you are transferring the call. When the person picks up the phone, explain briefly that you are transferring a call and what it is about. You might say something like, "I am transferring a call from a Mr. Jones who would like to know how to place an order." It is discourteous simply to say, "Transferring," and hang up.

27

Companies that receive a great many calls, particularly for information, do use an automated version of this procedure. An answering machine takes the call and informs the caller that all lines are busy, and to please hold. While annoying, this does not seem quite so rude as having a person refuse to listen to you. It is hardly different from getting a busy signal—you can hang up and call later, except that you will lose your "place in line."

Take Effective Messages

28

Garbled messages are the bane of businesses. The caller is not called back, or no one seems to know what the call was about. Names and numbers written incorrectly embarrass the person returning the call. Use "While You Were Out" message forms that help you take messages. If you do not have these forms, remember to note:

✓ name of person being called, and the correct pronunciation,

✓ date and time (AM or PM) of the call,

✓ caller's name, spelled correctly, title (Mr. Mrs., Ms.), and company,

✓ (pick one) "telephoned"—"urgent"—"will telephone again at (time)"—"please call"—"returned your call,"

✓ correct phone number, including area code and extension,

✓ content of the message the person gave.

After making notes read them to the caller to check the message's accuracy. The caller will be impressed at your thoroughness.

Learn to Screen Calls

You may be required to *screen* calls for your employer or supervisor. To **screen** calls is to sort out one kind of call from another. Your supervisor may wish to speak only to certain individuals. Your job would be to screen out all others. Screening calls requires tact and good judgement. Often you can help callers even if you cannot let them speak to the person whose calls you are screening. You can help by answering their questions or finding who in the company can help them, by taking their messages accurately, and by being courteous.

Transferring a call to another person or department may be all that is needed for some calls. Not all callers will know their way around your business, and you can help point them in the right direction. If the call cannot be transferred, take a clear, professional message. Do not promise when the call will be returned unless instructed to do so.

Screening may also require that you obtain the identity of the caller without necessarily putting the call through. For example, "One moment while I see if Mrs. Packer is free to talk with you. May I say who is calling?" It is important, if you are going to screen calls, that you and whomever you are screening for have a clear understanding of how calls will be handled so you avoid misunderstandings.

Exercise Tact

Often the person being called is simply unavailable. He or she may be in a meeting, out of the office, on another line. Politely explain that the person cannot come to the phone. If you know the person will be available in a few seconds, you can ask the caller to wait. If you know the person will be busy a long time, say so. If you know a good time to call back and have permission to give it, do so. You can ask when the person can return the call and take the information.

You do not need to be explicit in explaining that someone cannot answer the phone. The caller does not need to know that your boss is playing golf this afternoon or has gone to the dentist. It is sufficient to say only, "I'm sorry, Mr. Peterson is out of the office. Shall I have him return your call?" Use tact.

Developing Skills for Outbound Calls

Inbound calls are unpredictable. You cannot predict when the phone will ring or know who is calling or what the call is about. You control outbound calls, and it's your turn to be aware that, for another person, your call will be unpredictable.

You Are In Charge

A business call requires preparation and thought. Rarely, on a business phone, do you call others just to visit. You place business calls to accomplish certain purposes, and you will want to limit the time you spend on the phone, because both you and the person you are calling are busy working.

Be Considerate
The responsibility is with you, the caller, to be aware that now you are the interrupter. While the person you call has the right to ask you to

call back, many people feel a phone call must be responded to immediately whether they are receptive or not. The only courteous thing to do is to ask, "Am I reaching you at a good time?"

Place Your Own Call
Having someone place your calls is seldom acceptable. You may enjoy a sense of power having someone put a call through for you, but you send a message that your time is more valuable than that of the person being called. That person may conclude you are arrogant and inconsiderate. Putting through your own call shows interest and concern—invaluable assets in building solid business relationships. If you should be asked to place a call, use wording such as this:

> *Hello, I'm . . ., placing a call for Pat Jones to Mr. Orion. Is this Mr. Orion?*
>
> *Yes, it is.*
>
> *Thank you. Do you have a few minutes to talk with Mr. Orion, as he has some important matters to discuss?*
>
> *One minute please, Mr. Orion. I am connecting you with Mr. Jones.*

Before You Place Your Call

Prepare for the call. Jot down the points to cover, or questions to ask. Do whatever homework may be required—gather information, have pertinent materials at hand, review notes or correspondence relating to the topic. Anticipate questions. Have answers ready. Have clean notepaper. If returning a call, reread any message to refresh your memory.

Write down the name and number of the person you are to call. Do this even if you know her or him well—perhaps especially if you do. If you make many calls, it is easy to misdial. Perhaps you have just finished a call and absentmindedly redialed the same number. Or the number is similar to another you use often. Everyone who spends time on the phone, placing one call after the other, has had the experience of being momentarily mixed up, unable to remember who they called. Writing the name and number down protects you from these blunders.

Be Businesslike

You have read that a business phone is usually answered in three to five rings. You expect that it will be picked up in that time. You can ex-

30

tend the benefit of a doubt and let it ring longer, but not much longer. Someone should have answered, but if no one has after eight rings, hang up. There may be a reason the person cannot pick up and the continual ringing will annoy all within hearing.

Make Sure the Other Person Has Time
As you know, the ringing of the telephone is an interruption. Be sensitive to the possibility that the person called is involved in an important task and may not have the time to talk. Always ask politely if this is a convenient time. If it is not, make arrangements to call again.

State Your Purpose Right Away
Get to your point quickly. This does not mean to be rude. Be social and civil, but do not dawdle. If the person is a friend or business acquaintance, exchange pleasant preliminaries, inquire about business, and family, keeping it brief. When calling strangers, asking about their health or families would seem odd. Instead, your opening comments should provide background information about your company and your function within it to give the other person a context for what you will say.

31

Placing Special Calls

Long distance, conference, and international calls are used more frequently by businesses than by individuals, particularly conference and international calls.

Long Distance Calls

You have already read about long distance calls. A long distance call is any call out of your local area. If it is made within your area code it requires only a "1" before the seven digit number; outside your area code, you must dial 1 + area code + local number. (Again, this may vary, but the basic pattern holds throughout the country.)

There are some other things to consider when placing a long distance call, especially if you have to call across the country. You need to be aware what time it is in the place you are calling. Say you are working in Atlanta, Georgia, and need some information from a company in Sacramento, California. You decide to call when you start work at 9 a.m. so you can have the day to work on the information that you will receive. Of course, no one will answer the phone out in Sacramento because it is only 6 a.m. when you call.

The 48 contiguous states are divided into four **time zones**, each one an hour earlier moving from east to west. These are Eastern, Central, Mountain, and Pacific. There are an additional two time zones for Alaska and a third for Hawaii. Canada shares our basic four zones, but has an additional zone to the east for its maritime provinces. Mexico shares three: Central, Mountain, and Pacific. To call Mexico, you have to use international telephone call procedures. To call Canada you dial 1 + area code + local number, just as you would a long distance number within this country.

The west coast is three hours behind the east coast. The time to call California from Georgia is in the afternoon. Being aware of time zone differences will stop you from making calls at inappropriate times and help you plan any work dependent upon such calls. As you read, at the front of the phone book is an area code and time zone map that tells you how to calculate the time elsewhere.

Conference Calls

A **conference call**, or "teleconferencing," makes it possible for three or more people in different places to take part in the same call. Your office may be equipped with phones that can handle conference calls. If not, teleconferencing can be set up by an operator. You tell the operator when to make the call, and the names and numbers of the people you wish to participate. Usually, you call an "800" number to reach the phone company "teleconferencing coordinator" who describes the types of calls available and takes a reservation for your call.

When arranging a conference call, make appointments for all the conferees to be standing by at the appointed time.

International Calls

From many locations in the United States, international calls can be dialed directly. You first dial an **international access code**, which for calls from this country is 011. Otherwise, from any location you can reach an operator who will help you to make an international call.

A page in the front of the phone book lists codes for many foreign countries and cities. The hourly difference between your time zone and others is indicated by a number (a minus sign indicates earlier time). To call Paris, France, from the Eastern Time Zone of the United States (standard time), you would find the country code is 33, the city code is 1, and the time difference is plus six hours.

To place international calls you need the country and city codes and the local number. To dial directly, you dial the international access

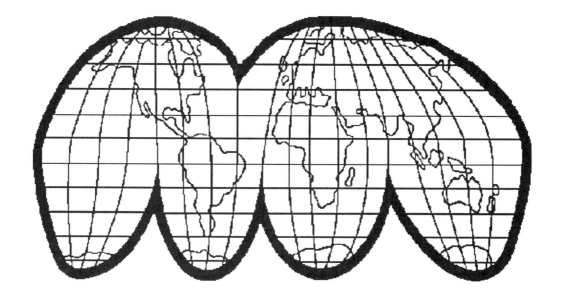

You can dial directly to nearly anywhere in the world today. To do so, you must first dial an international access code. Then you must dial the country and city code plus the individual number. On all long distance calls remember to check time zones.

number "011" then the other numbers: 011 + two- or three-digit country code + one-to-five-digit city code + local number. In areas without international direct dialing, dial "0" and the operator places the call.

Working with Answering Machines

Answering machines are common today. They are impersonal and, for that reason, many callers dislike them and decline to leave messages. Always accept the recorded invitation to leave a message. There are good reasons for doing so. Take advantage of the machine to leave a positive, upbeat message with your name and number. For example:

> *First of all, I want to thank you for providing me with the opportunity to leave a message. My name is (name) and I'm with (company). The reason for my call is (give reason) and I look forward to your call. My number is (number) and the best time to reach me is (time). Thank you.*

Since most people receive negative feedback about having a machine, by thanking them for providing it you put them in a positive mood. Notice that you thank them *before* you give your name and number.

The recipient will appreciate that you left a message. Further, most people return calls, so you can usually wait for the return call rather

34

Some people try to be humorous with their phone answering machine and have such recorded messages as, "Please leave your message after the dog barks." Although you may laugh, you still need to be prepared to leave a clear and accurate message.

Speak in a normal, clear tone when leaving a message, just as if you were talking to the person.

If you use an answering machine at home, avoid having messages that say you are out and when you will return. There is no point in broadcasting the fact that your house will be empty for a period of time to anyone who happens to call.

A good answering message is "You have reached (company name and phone number). Although no one can come to the phone right now, please leave your name and number and we will return your call as soon as possible."

than spending your time calling back. If the person does not call within a day, of course, make another attempt to contact the person.

Preparation Counts

Sometimes people are flustered by an answering machine. They either cannot leave a message or leave a garbled one. If you have prepared your call, you will be able to leave a brief, coherent message. If you have the person's name written down and a note with the key points to make, you will feel confident and at ease responding to the mechanical invitation. More important, you will leave the message you wish to leave.

Possible Responses

Here are a few typical messages you might hear from an answering machine and some suggested responses that you can use as guides.

Machine: Hello, you have reached Editorial Ideas. We are unable to come to the phone right now. After the beep, please leave your name, phone, and message. We will return your call as soon as possible. Thank you for calling.

Caller: This is Sharon Smith of Diamond Composition at 212/798-0000. Please call me today about the proofs for your book.

Machine: Hello. You have reached the Anthropology Department at Western University. No one can come to the phone at the moment. Please leave a message and someone will get back to you shortly.

Caller: Hello, this is Bill Oster calling for Professor Kanter. I'm calling to schedule my makeup exam. My number is 404-1111.

Machine: You have reached Smith and Turgeon Engineering Association. We value your call so after the tone, please leave your name, company, phone number, and time and date of your call. You may leave a two-minute message. Thank you for calling.

Caller: Hello, this is Alice Williams from Johnson Electrical Company, 517/456-7890. It is 2 pm, Wednesday, March 3. We have prepared the estimates for your electrical work and are mailing them to you today. If you have questions about them, please call either me or Bill Schaefer. We look forward to your reaction.

Quiz Questions

1. List three kinds of operator assisted calls.

2. What is the best way to learn how to pronounce a name?

3. What are some ways to end a telephone call gracefully?

4. What can you do when you receive a call from a talkative person?

5. List at least four skills for inbound calls.

6. Why is it better to make your own calls?

7. What should you take into consideration when you place outbound calls and how should you prepare to call?

8. List the skills for handling all calls professionally.

9. Should you leave messages on answering machines? Explain your answer.

Discussion Questions

1. Discuss using first and last names and titles in business telephone calls. What do you have to consider when deciding which name or title to use on the phone?

2. Discuss screening calls. What are some things to consider? Brainstorm about potentially awkward situations and how to handle them tactfully.

Activities

1. This activity will help you learn what professional telephone skills others appreciate. Equip yourself with a pad of paper and a pen, and ask your friends and family members to tell you about their pet telephone peeves. One friend may say, "I hate it when you answer the phone and the caller says 'Who's this?'" Once you have a list of peeves, review the chapter and determine which procedures apply to each peeve and write it down.

2. Without placing them, practice making the following calls. Look up and write down a procedure for each, include what time or range of times you would place the call, and, if you can, figure out what the calls would cost.

   ■ Obtain the number of Metro-Goldwyn Mayer in Los Angeles, California, from Des Moines, Iowa.

   ■ Call Victoria, British Columbia, from Orlando, Florida.

   ■ Call Rome, Italy, from Ohio during business hours.

   ■ Call your United States Representative at the representative's office both in your home state and in Washington, DC.

   ■ Set up a conference call from your location in Princeton, New Jersey, with conferees in Dallas, Texas, Salt Lake City, Utah, and Mexico City, Mexico.

Chapter Four

Listening Effectively

Upon completing this chapter you will be able to:

① *recognize the difference between hearing and listening,*

② *use three skills to ensure active listening on the telephone,*

③ *use three techniques for retaining more of what you hear on the telephone,*

④ *overcome external and internal obstacles to listening.*

Effective communication between two people requires that both have the opportunity to *speak*, which means both must also *listen*. When handling an inbound call, you immediately identify yourself, and then your important task becomes to LISTEN. Even when you place a call and will do most of the talking, you still must listen if the call is to be successful. In this chapter, you will learn techniques to be a good listener.

Businesses that encourage their employees to listen improve their sales and reputations for good service. If you are acquainted with a business organization that is the object of frequent complaints about its poor communication, the chances are that its people have not mastered listening skills. They may be so eager to get their message across they do not have the time to hear what anyone is saying.

Recognizing How Hearing and Listening Differ

The sense of *hearing* is something people are born with. *Listening* is a learned skill.

✓ **Hearing** refers to the reception of sounds, the physical act of sound waves entering the ear and brain.

✓ **Listening** means interpreting and understanding the sounds that enter your ear.

Whether you want to or not, you *hear* sounds made around you, although often without being conscious of them. Your conscious response to sounds is *listening*. Listening requires paying attention to sounds. You interpret not just words but all sounds. Sometimes you merely identify the sound; sometimes the sound is associated with something else in your consciousness to which you may respond physically or emotionally. A telephone ringing, for example, creates a sense of urgency in most people and they respond by answering it.

A Four-Part Process

Listening involves four steps on the part of the hearer:

1. the physical act of sensing or hearing,

2. interpreting the sound,

3. evaluating the data and deciding how to use it,

4. responding.

Compensate for Lack of Visual Clues

39

Listening is important in telephoning because it is the only way to obtain *feedback*. **Feedback** is the response of the other person, which can include a direct spoken reply, as well as other clues, verbal or visual. You need feedback so as to know what the other person thinks and feels to guide you in deciding what to do next.

On the telephone you lack visual feedback. You cannot look at people over the telephone to see if they are paying attention. The person on the other end of the phone cannot tell if you are being distracted by a note on your memo pad, nodding your head or shaking it. You must rely on the clues contained in the vocal expressions.

A good listener interprets all the aspects of voice and language that you have read about: the speaker's pitch, emphasis, tone, rate, volume, inflection, as well as the words. Each of these aspects conveys messages. A loud volume conveys something different from a low whisper and a fast rate of speech suggests something different from a slow rate. Listen to these signals for clues to the message being sent and thus compensate for not being able to see the visual clues that aid understanding and communicating in face-to-face conversations.

Developing Skills for Active Listening

Active listening involves responding and encouraging the other to speak. Active listeners do not passively absorb sound. They participate. Active listeners keep their minds focused on the conversation. The sections below describe ways to be an active listener.

Respond

You can be an active listener by using your voice. That seems a contradiction: if you are talking you are not listening. However, by speaking you can tell the other person that you are indeed listening. An important part of any communication is to make the other person feel listened to. This is especially necessary on the telephone.

Think of someone you know who is a good listener. What does that person do to make you feel listened to? If you think about it, you might find that the person who makes you feel you are being listened to has these characteristics:

✓ looks at you when you talk,

✓ nods, smiles, or otherwise reacts appropriately with facial expression and body language,

✓ asks pertinent questions at appropriate moments,

✓ makes fitting comments on what you say to encourage you.

The first two, which are visual clues, cannot be given over the telephone. Thus, an important part of active listening on the telephone is responding vocally, with words, sounds, or whole sentences. The response can be as simple as "um-hm," "I see," "ok;" or as complicated as a carefully thought out reply to a question. They tell the person you *hear* them and are *listening*. They are called "interest comments."

Response is Feedback

Feedback—the detailed response—lets the other person know that you are *listening*, that you have understood. What response you make, of course, depends a great deal on the circumstances. You may agree, disagree, ask for or give information. Important feedback includes repeating what you heard so as to give the other person the opportunity to correct any misunderstanding. In business, such feedback is useful because it can prevent major, and sometimes costly, misunderstandings. Perhaps you have had the experience of a waiter repeating your order. Or when you buy merchandise by phone, the representative reads all the information back.

Respond with Questions

A good response is to ask questions. Knowing when to ask questions, knowing what kind to ask, and picking up on responses to the questions requires careful listening. Asking questions helps you to listen.

Ask polite, low-key questions to find out what the other person is thinking and whether what you have said is clear to him or her. Asking questions not only shows that you are listening, it also helps the person you are talking with listen as well. When asking questions do

Let's look at the following telephone conversation and identify message, response, and feedback.

"George, its good to hear from you." [message]

"Well, its good to hear from you, Ellen." [response]

"I couldn't get back to you sooner because I've been on vacation." [message]

"I see. Well, the reason I was calling was to talk to you about the Springfield project. We got the go ahead and we'd like you to be involved." [response, new message]

"Great. What time frame are we looking at?" [response, new message]

"We'd like to be under way by October." [response]

"That works for me." [feedback]

"Then what I'd like to do is sit down with you some time in the next week and go over the details." [message].

"That'd be fine. What about lunch Tuesday?" [response, new message]

As the conversation progresses, each new message becomes a response and a kind of feedback to the previous message.

not sound as if you are interrogating someone or pushing. However, do not miss opportunities to ask questions and thus allow misunderstandings to stand, or leave doubts in the other person's mind.

Gesture

Being active physically helps you to be an active listener. It may seem odd to suggest making physical gestures on the phone, but even though the other person cannot see what you do, what you do helps you listen as well as respond. Some examples are, when you agree, nod and smile, or shake your head in sympathy. Using gestures when you speak helps add feeling to your voice.

Summarize

In any business communication, on the telephone or face to face, you will find it is useful to summarize conversations. Summarizing is a form of feedback and is a key listening device. If you have been providing feedback in the course of the conversation, then summarizing is the natural final step. Just briefly restate the important points; double check facts, especially any needed for follow-up work; and then conclude by stating what the agreed upon action or the next step will be. Doing this prevents errors of the "but I thought I told you" or the "I don't remember you saying that" variety.

Using Techniques to Improve Retention

42

In an earlier chapter you read about how easy it is to become distracted on the phone. Listening on the phone requires you to focus on the voice in your receiver so that when you hang up you can remember what you talked about. Not seeing the person can make this difficult to do.

Think for a moment about how you remember things. **Retention** , or the capacity to remember, often has many aspects besides the one associated with what you heard on a given occasion. You may retain sights, smells, and flavors, even the temperature or texture of something you touched. These create a **matrix**, a distinct situation or background, against which your memory is placed. Any one of these memories may be triggered and all the other memories rush back, too, each helping the other recreate the whole occasion for you.

When you are on the phone, your range of sensory input is greatly reduced. In the workplace, all your phone calls will probably have the same matrix or background: your desk, your phone, the people coming and going near you will remain the same for call after call. There will be little outside you that will help you remember what makes one call different from another.

You can, however, compensate for this by creating mental images as you listen and by taking notes.

Create Mental Images

When you listen to the radio, you hear the disc jockey and the reporter talk, hear their tones of voice, their choices of words, and unconsciously develop a mental picture of them. It might be a picture based on someone else you know who sounds like the person on the radio. It might be a picture based on your preconceived notions that someone with a voice like that will be tall and have dark hair, or be short and blond. This activity can be made more deliberate and put to good use on the phone to help you retain more of what you hear. Forming mental images as you listen, or speak, helps you remember.

If you are giving a prospective client instructions for finding your company, it can be useful to imagine yourself driving along the road the client will have to take. Mentally recreating the trip, you can "see" and can thus point out landmarks to look for before making turns. This will alert you to what might be a confusing intersection that you would want to caution the client about, for example.

When you are listening, turn the process around, actively develop mental pictures of the things or processes being described. When the discussion centers on ideas and concepts for which there are no concrete images you can call up, use your mental imaging to visualize the other person speaking, or try to see the words in your mind.

43

Take Notes

The benefit of notetaking is that it makes mental images visible. Reviewing your notes triggers associated thoughts, which help to recreate the conversation in your memory. What you write down depends on whether you are receiving or placing a call. It depends on whether each of your calls is unique or whether they all accomplish the same basic purpose.

Chapter Two discussed taking messages and provided a list of what you need to write down to take an effective message. If you are taking notes for yourself, you are, in effect, taking a message for yourself and will need much the same information. As you read, making notes directly on memos or correspondence that relate to the phone call is a good idea.

If your telephone calls are all very similar you may find that your company provides you with forms for notetaking—for example, order blanks or telephone record sheets. If there are none, and you notice a similarity in your calls, you could develop your own note form and always have a supply of duplicated forms on your desk.

Good notes give you something to refer to when you summarize the conversation. Because you are not frantically trying to remember all that was said, you can take a moment to get perspective and comprehend the whole conversation, ask any questions that occur to you, and be free to relate to the other person as a person, not just a voice.

Notetaking Shortcuts

As with all notetaking, it is unreasonable to expect to write down everything. It is better to concentrate on the conversation than to become absorbed in the notetaking. A few key words and phrases should be all you need. When you hang up, you can return to your notes and add the details you think you will need. Do write down vital statistics, though, such as model numbers, names, addresses, and phone numbers. Below are some tips for taking notes quickly, based in part on a system developed by Dr. Gregg Condon. Remember, though, that these are suggestions. Use what works best for you.

Use Abbreviations

Use abbreviations and symbols—as long as you do not forget what they stand for. Commonly used abbreviations and symbols—"FYI" which stands for "for your information" or "#" for number—are safest. Your company's jargon might include commonly used abbreviations or symbols for product lines or policies and procedure, which you can use confidently. If you develop a set of abbreviations, consider making a key to refer to with the abbreviation and its meaning written down.

Words of two or more syllables can be easily abbreviated. A common way is to eliminate the vowels, leaving only the consonants: the word *consonants* becomes "cnsnts," *vowels* becomes "vwls." Another way is to record only the first or the important syllable: "frequently" becomes *freq.*, "psychology" becomes *psych.*, "attend" becomes *att.*

Be alert for the danger in this system. "Rel," for example, could stand for *related, relationship, religion, relapse, release, relevant.*

To avoid this, use only those abbreviations whose meaning will be obvious to you later, from the abbreviation itself or from the context. There is no point trying to save a few seconds when writing notes and discovering later you must spent a lot of time trying to decipher what you wrote. Never, by the way, abbreviate or take shortcuts when writing someone's name. Spell it out.

A pen or pencil and a notepad are good listening tools. Taking notes can help you focus on what is being said.

If you use abbreviations, do not eliminate silent letters (see below). This can make the word unrecognizable.

Use Telegraphic Style

Use the **telegraphic style** for taking notes. That means to eliminate **function words**—prepositions, articles, auxiliary verbs (the, an, of, be, do, have)—and other secondary words wherever possible. Copy editors use the telegraphic style writing headlines: "Senate kills new tax law." In this example the full sentence would ready "The Senate kills a new tax law."

Do Not Write Silent Letters

Another notetaking technique is to eliminate silent letters—letters that are not pronounced. For example:

day = da	see = se
leave = lev	settle = setl
feature = fetur	trouble = trubl
listen = lisn	bought = bot

45

A little practice will quickly accustom you to this style of writing.

Write Sounds

Use **phonetic spelling**—that is, writing the word as it sounds to you without worrying about the correct spelling. Phonetic spellings are usually shorter than standard ones: "phone" spelled phonetically is "fon," which saves you two letters. This may not seem like a lot, but over a period of time, such savings can significantly speed up your notetaking. Also, you are not slowing down to make sure of the spelling. The dangers, of course, are that you might not recognize the word later or that you might use the phonetic spelling in written communication. When you spell phonetically be sure you write enough to remember what the word is.

Overcoming Listening Roadblocks

Most of the time, it is not practical to *listen* to every sound you hear. Modern life is full of noise. In fact, one aspect of some mental illness is the inability to filter out sound or to distinguish between the sounds to which attention must be paid and those that can be safely ignored. Listening to everything can drive a person to distraction, so you develop unconscious methods of ignoring some kinds of sound. You also create conscious mental roadblocks to listening.

There are two kinds of listening roadblocks: external and internal. The external ones are sometimes outside your control, but in general can be overcome easily. The internal roadblocks are all within your control, but they can sometimes be difficult to overcome. You might not even be aware that some exist.

External Obstacles to Listening

At times, external factors beyond your control make listening difficult. These include such things as a poor connection or background noise (from office machines, such as typewriters or other phones inside, or from construction work or traffic outside). You do not have control of these nuisances, but there are ways to deal with them.

If you have a poor connection, acknowledge it right away rather than struggle through an entire call. It quickly becomes annoying when you keep repeating:

46

> *Excuse me, I can't hear you. Could you say that again?*

Instead simply say:

> *Excuse me. We seem to have a poor connection, Mr. Willard. Please hang up and I will call you right back.*

Sometimes the connection is poor only for one of the two parties. If you sense that the person you have called is straining to hear, you might ask:

> *Mrs. Noyes, is my voice coming through clearly? If not, perhaps we have a bad connection. Why don't you hang up and I will call you right back?*

You should never suggest that the person has a hearing problem. Often the person will tell you if that is the case. If the person tells you he or she has a hearing problem, or if you sense it is the case, try raising the volume of your voice slightly; or, better still, lower your pitch.

Clutter—papers to be filed, stacks of unfinished projects, unnecessary objects in your work area—makes it harder to listen, and constantly reminds you of things to do. Your mind is distracted by the clutter.

Keep your work area free of clutter. You must have several items on it, of course. Have those items neatly organized so they will be less likely to distract you as you listen on the phone.

Internal Obstacles

Internal obstacles to good listening are almost always mental. That is, they are part of your thought process. Some internal roadblocks derive from physical aspects, however. If you are not feeling well or had a late night, you may find it hard to concentrate. On such days, you must make a special effort to concentrate.

Concentration, patience, and interest are all internal factors affecting your ability to listen that you can develop and control to some degree. We all have internal listening roadblocks—habits of listening or not listening—that have developed from childhood.

A listening roadblock can be based on fear. People who have difficulty with numbers might find themselves freezing mentally when they hear a lot of statistics. Feeling anxious about being able to cope with these statistics, they do not hear the numbers clearly. A defensive person, unable to take criticism, will not hear a complaint clearly. Someone who resents authority may not be able to listen carefully to instructions.

Another type of listening roadblock results from anticipation. Familiar with the subject and thinking you know what the other person will say, you stop listening. Your mind races on ahead of what it hears and anticipates, often incorrectly, what the person will say.

47

Not a Simple Process

Work to become aware of your listening roadblocks. Then try to eliminate them or compensate for them. This is not easy. Developing the active listening skills described above is a big step toward overcoming them. If you are actively listening, you reduce the chance that a mental roadblock is preventing you from receiving information.

Keep track of times when it turns out that you had gotten some information wrong from a caller. These could show a pattern that will help you identify an internal obstacle.

There is no sure way to eliminate internal obstacles to listening. Some you never will. However, by being aware, striving to be an active listener, and keeping track of the times when the information did not get through to you, you will overcome some of these obstacles.

The Question Behind the Question

Not everyone is capable of stating clearly what he or she wants or needs. Sometimes this happens because the caller has a fear of annoying someone or a fear of how he or she will be perceived. Sometimes the problem occurs because the caller does not have enough information to ask the right question.

A helpful professional will make an effort to look for the question behind the question. For example, someone purchasing a product might ask, "What happens if it doesn't work right?" or "What happens if I don't like it?" More than likely the real question this person wants answered is, "What kind of service, returns policy, guarantees, and so on do you offer?" You, as an active listener, can clarify by giving a thorough explanation of these points.

Messages must overcome many obstacles in the mind before they can be understood and acted upon.

48

Getting at the questions behind the question almost always requires responding with questions that explore the caller's concerns and meanings.

Evaluation and Judgment

One telephone call—one business transaction—does not stand alone. It is part of a whole system of communication. It is easy to deal with each call in turn and meet the particular need stated or solve the immediate problem. It is not so easy to understand all the calls in their larger context.

Use evaluation and judgment to listen for patterns as you answer the phone or make calls, which helps you see the bigger picture of your company's work. To do this, consider as you listen:

✓ How can this information be used best?

✓ Is this challenge like another you have overcome?

✓ Is there something you can do to overcome these challenges before they affect your clients and customers?

✓ Is there a body of information that many people seem to need?

✓ How else can this information be shared?

These questions will not only help you overcome internal obstacles to listening, but help you to spot and deal with challenges and develop better communication between your company and its customers.

Quiz Questions

1. Effective communication between two people requires that each have a chance to do what two things?

2. How is *listening* different from *hearing*?

3. List the four parts of the listening process.

4. What does *active listening* involve?

5. What two activities help you to retain the information that you hear?

6. When you have a bad telephone connection, what is the best thing to do?

7. Is there a connection between a neat desk and effective listening?

8. What is meant by "the question behind the question?"

49

Discussion Questions

1. Describe what active listeners do.

2. Cite four shortcuts that help you take notes rapidly and easily.

3. Describe some internal roadblocks to listening that people need to recognize if they are to be good listeners. Is there any easy way to deal with such roadblocks?

Activities

1. This activity allows you to practice making mental images. Go to the library or look at home for a book that contains instructions for making or fixing something, preferably a book which has no illustrations—a cookbook, car repair manual, sewing or knitting directions, instructions for building a piece of furniture, or a manual for operating a piece of equipment.

   Read the directions once quickly. Close the book, and try to visualize following the directions. Make a mental note of how clear the instructions seem to be. Reread the instructions, and now, as you read them, visualize yourself following each step. Make as complete a mental image as you can, even picturing yourself in the place where you would carry out the process, the time of day, who might be with you, and so on. Now close the book again and repeat the process mentally. Do you have a clearer image of it this time?

W e do not see ourselves as others see us, nor do we *hear* ourselves as others hear us—especially over the phone. How your telephone voice sounds to others depends on a number of factors:

✓ how you pronounce words,

✓ your tone, pitch, speed, volume, emphasis,

✓ the quality of the equipment.

On the telephone, the quality of your voice is particularly important, because, as you have read, your listeners have only your voice and the words you use to form their impression of you and your company. You do not have gestures and facial expressions to convey your message. Your voice has to do the whole job. In this job, not only are the words you choose important, but the way you speak them.

Realizing How Pronunciation and Articulation Differ

Being effective on the telephone requires that you say words clearly and correctly. That involves *pronunciation* and *articulation*. Correct **pronunciation** means voicing the standard, accepted sounds in each word. Good **articulation** means producing the sounds clearly, distinctly and smoothly. Articulation is also sometimes called **enunciation**.

For example, the correct *pronunciation* of seine (a net used in fishing) is sane, not sen or seen. The word fishing is well *articulated* (or *enunciated*) when the final *g* is pronounced (not fishin). In regard to pronunciation, there is a correct and an incorrect way to say a word. There is no correct articulation as such; words are either clearly or poorly articulated. Your goal is to combine good articulation with correct pronunciation.

2. The only way to improve your listening skills is to practice them. During the next two weeks, keep a log of all your telephone calls. Keep a pad of paper and a pencil next to the phone. Each time you answer the phone write down the date and time. During the calls, practice your professional telephone skills but pay special attention to active listening and listening for retention. Be alert to the need for response and feedback; summarize conversations when appropriate; gesture at appropriate moments; take notes; create mental images while you are listening and use these to help remember what is being said.

When the call is over, and the memory of it fresh, review the conversation and evaluate how well you did. Note in the log the nature of the call and write down the professional telephone skills you used. As the weeks progress, try to be aware of any changes in your telephone habits, and note them. At the end of the two-week period, review your log and write a brief self-evaluation on changes and improvements in your professional telephone skills.

Chap

Speaking
Clearly and Corre

Upon completing this chapter you wi

① *recognize the difference between pron and articulation,*

② *use techniques that help you maint articulation and pronunciation,*

③ *improve your vocal expression by red its five characteristics,*

④ *eliminate outside factors that can inte your speaking quality.*

Pronunciation

People expect to hear words pronounced in certain ways. When they hear words mispronounced, they are distracted and become inattentive. Such inattention can prevent you from conveying your message. If you say something important, but mispronounce a word or name, your listener's concentration is broken. Your point is lost.

Correct *pronunciation* involves selecting the proper *vowel* and *consonant* sounds and stressing the proper syllables. You might enunciate a word clearly, but pronounce it incorrectly. You might articulate the word "often" clearly, but mispronounce it by sounding the *t*, which should be silent. Or you might pronounce a difficult word correctly, but articulate it so sloppily that you cannot be understood.

Vowels are a, e, i, o, and u. **Consonants** are all the other letters. You will read more below on articulating vowels and consonants.

Use a Dictionary

A dictionary is necessary equipment if you want to pronounce words correctly. It gives not only the meanings of words but also their correct pronunciations. Every word is written out with pronunciation symbols to tell you how each letter or combination of letters should sound. There will also be a pronunciation key, which gives examples of each letter in use in an illustration word. The pronunciation key is often located at the bottom of each page.

For example, "a" can be pronounced as in "pay," "pat," "father," or "care." Each of these slightly different sounds is shown by the letter "a" with symbols attached to it.

Each time you learn a new word, look it up in the dictionary

53

Every word in the dictionary has a pronunciation guide. A different symbol is used for each sound. For example, the letter "a" is pronounced many different ways; by adding marks to the letter the dictionary distinguishes among pronunciations. A key to interpret the symbols is also provided. This is how a key might distinguish among pronunciations for *a*:

a: pat   ā: pay
â: care   ä: father

Below is a pronunciation guide for the word "enunciate." The *italicized* syllable is given the main stress; the apostrophe shows secondary stress. Symbols vary from one dictionary to the next, but the basic idea is the same.

enunciate: i-*nun*-sē-at'

to be sure you are giving it the correct pronunciation. Even if you have heard the word pronounced before, double check, because there is always a chance you heard it mispronounced.

Tips for Pronouncing

Here are tips for pronouncing words correctly. They reflect the five most common causes of mispronouncing a word.

✓ STRESS THE RIGHT SYLLABLE: In the words *preferable*, *comparable*, and *abdomen*, for example, the stress belongs on the first syllable (PREF-er-a-ble, COM-par-a-ble, AB-do-men), yet many people stress the second.

✓ DO NOT OMIT SOUNDS: Be aware of such sounds as the first *r* in *library*, which is frequently dropped, but should be pronounced.

✓ DO NOT SUBSTITUTE SOUNDS: Do not substitute *b* for *p* in *Baptist* or *w* for *wh* in *why*, for example.

✓ DO NOT REVERSE SOUNDS: An example of this would be saying *prespiration* for *perspiration*.

✓ DO NOT ADD SOUNDS: Do not add *r* to *idea*, so that it becomes *idear*, or *y* to *column*, so that it becomes *colyumn*.

Articulation

You want to articulate clearly to be understood and not sound sloppy, lazy, or inconsiderate. At the same time, you do not want to sound unnatural. Over-articulated speech can sound tense, irritated or forced. Striking a balance takes practice and patience, but is worth the effort.

Work on your articulation, making sure that you enunciate words and names distinctly and speak smoothly. Having an idea of how the sounds of speech are formed can help you in this endeavor. In this section, you will read how speech sounds are formed, as well as tips for making your own telephone voice clear, understandable and smooth.

Physical characteristics—mouth and teeth—affect articulation, and so can your emotional state, use of medication, and alcohol. Clear articulation can also be learned along with language. There are regional and cultural differences in articulation which we call accents.

Physical Effects on Articulation

Our breathing system is also our speech-producing system. Here is a simplified explanation of how it works.

✔ Air passes through the **pharynx**, a double-duty passageway shared by the eating system.

✔ The pharynx is connected to both the **esophagus**, the food pipe that leads to the stomach, and to the **trachea**, the air pipe leading to the lungs.

✔ At the top of the trachea is the **larynx**, the human voice box.

The folds of tissue that close the larynx are the **vocal cords**. When stretched tight, they vibrate, producing sound waves in the air coming from the lungs through the larynx. As sounds from the larynx travel out through the mouth, they are modified by the movement and placement of the lips, tongue, teeth, and jaws. The place and manner in which they are modified determines what particular sounds they will become.

Vowel sounds are not blocked by tongue, teeth or lips, but they are *shaped* by the tongue and lips. For example, narrowing the back of the mouth with the tongue produces a different sound from that made by opening it wide. Vowel sounds are part of every word.

Consonants are produced by temporarily blocking or obstructing the flow of air from the lungs. If you do not say these sounds clearly, your speech will be indistinct. It is especially important to move your tongue and lips so as to make your consonants clearly.

Many people mispronounce the word "picture" as "PIT-shur." To pronounce it correctly, the tongue must go from the back of the throat, where the *k* sound is made, to the front of the mouth, where the *t* sound is made, very rapidly. People often slur over or drop the *k* sound to save the effort of enunciating such different sounds so close together.

The sound you produce is partly determined by the shape of your face and mouth and the placement of your teeth. It is also determined by how you hear, because you repeat sounds as you hear them.

55

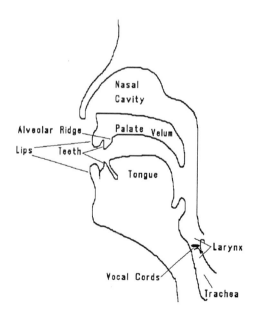

The sounds of speech are formed in the *vocal tract*, which begins at the trachea and reaches to the lips.

Other Influences on Articulation

Tension or stress can produce physical changes in the mouth that can affect articulation. If you are tense, you may unconsciously tighten your jaw or clench your teeth and sound is altered. In the chapter on stress and the telephone, you will read about relaxation techniques to keep tension from affecting your voice.

Certain medications, drugs, and alcohol affect your speech. They can also impair your thinking, which affects how well you speak.

The region or country in which you grew up affects your articulation. Dialects and accents can be pleasant to listen to and provide a relief from standard broadcast English. If you have a regional or foreign accent, however, be sure that the person with whom you are conversing on the phone understands you. Consider slowing your rate of speech (see below) and being aware of challenging sounds and words.

Building Careful Articulation

Physical and cultural effects on articulation aside, there are often bad personal habits of articulation and enunciation that can be corrected. Good articulation comes from concentrating on what you are saying and deciding to speak clearly. By listening to a tape recording of your voice and by having a teacher or friend help you critique your articulation you can become aware of the words you need to relearn.

If poor articulation comes from habits of lazy enunciation, slurring, or omitting sounds, awareness and practice will probably be all that is needed to correct it. Often such habits are related to a particular set of sounds: saying "dint" instead of "didn't" or "wunt" instead of "wouldn't." In these cases, the habit is omitting the second "d" sound.

While you want to say each sound clearly and distinctly, you do not want to sound artificial. Sometimes saying sounds very distinctly sounds artificial, particularly over the telephone. Speak naturally into the mouthpiece; do not accentuate sounds in an effort to say them distinctly. Say consonants clearly, yet not too distinctly.

Improving Vocal Expression

Vocal expression—the sound of your voice—refers to its _tone, pitch, rate of speech, volume,_ and use of _emphasis._ If someone has an irritating voice, it is usually because of a problem with one of these five characteristics. You give a great deal of meaning to words by the _vocal expression_ you use speaking them.

You develop your normal vocal expression as you grow. It is shaped by family and culture. Members of one family may always shout at one another. With them, the raised volume does not carry the emotional impact that it might for persons raised in a family where everyone is taught to speak quietly. Vocal expression also originates in as well as conveys your attitudes and emotions.

Tone of Voice

To a large extent, your tone of voice determines how well you project courtesy and a positive image. In Chapter Seven, you will learn more about projecting a positive image and about how your tone of voice can be affected by your unconscious thoughts, moods and emotions. **Tone of voice** specifically refers to the emotional quality of your voice.

57

Tone Conveys Feelings
Tone conveys feelings and attitudes; it indicates whether you are pleased or angry, enthusiastic or weary, friendly or hostile. As a child, you could often tell by your parents' tone when they said your name whether they were annoyed or pleased. You no doubt have heard some-one say something like, "Watch out for the teacher today, I can tell by the tone of her voice she's in a bad mood."

Your listeners can detect your feelings just by listening to your tone. They detect your alertness, your enthusiasm for your job, your confidence in yourself and in your company. They also detect listlessness, lack of interest, and lack of knowledge. Your tone of voice should project enthusiasm and interest in the person with whom you are speaking.

Put a Smile On It
One way to assure having a pleasant tone is to smile when you talk on the phone. How you shape the borders of your mouth affects the tone of your voice. When you smile, you create a pleasant and positive tone that conveys friendliness rather than a strictly business approach, en-thusiasm rather than boredom, energy rather than fatigue, and inter-est in the listener rather than a "just doing my job" attitude. On a bad day, when outside factors worry and annoy you, you need to maintain a cheerful tone. Consciously putting a smile on your face will help you to do this.

A smile makes you sound not only more cheerful and pleasant, but also more confident. You want to convey self-confidence when speaking on the phone. Even if you may not feel quite confident in yourself, you can be convincing to your listener by making a conscious effort to smile as you speak. A smile on your face puts confidence in your voice.

Be Real
As with many other vocal characteristics, you may have learned from your family to speak with a certain tone, of which you are unaware. To

become aware of how you sound, tape record your voice in a conversation with a friend. Listen to it. Have your teacher or a friend help you critique your voice. You may find that although you use courteous and helpful words, and even feel you _want_ to be courteous and helpful, your tone of voice is not conveying this.

While avoiding irritability, condescension, and disinterest, do not err in the other extreme and end up with a tone of voice that conveys gushiness, insincerity, or ultra-smoothness. Be genuine. Be yourself.

Pitch

58

Pitch is how high or low—squeaky or rumbly—a voice is. It refers to highness and lowness, as in musical notes on a scale. To some extent, pitch is determined by age or gender: children have higher pitch than adults, women have higher pitch than men. Other factors also affect pitch: smokers often have lower pitch than nonsmokers; someone stressed is likely to have a higher pitch than someone relaxed. You cannot accurately hear your voice's pitch because the sound is altered as it resonates in your head.

Pitch and Image

People unconsciously project certain images depending on the pitch of their voice: a woman with a high "little-girl" voice will not be taken as seriously as she would if she used a stronger, lower pitched voice; nor will a man with a high, whiney voice be considered as seriously as he would with a deep, resonant voice.

A presidential election campaign demonstrated the importance of the image projected by vocal expression. The winner was coached to lower his pitch and speak more slowly to appear "presidential." Almost everyone can benefit from dropping his or her voice to a slightly lower pitch.

A Natural Pitch

We all have a natural pitch at which we are most comfortable. Speaking at this natural level produces no strain on the vocal cords to mar the quality of the voice. Try to stay close to your natural pitch. To do so, you should be aware that there are some things that can cause your pitch to rise or fall, which can make your voice become unpleasant.

Eating, drinking, smoking, and tension can adversely affect your pitch. Smiling can improve your pitch, which is another reason to smile when talking on the telephone.

A smile can raise your pitch level by one or even two notes. Tension causes your throat to tighten, which produces a very high, unpleasant pitch. You will read of ways to reduce tension in Chapter Eight.

Rate of Speech

Rate of speech, how quickly you speak your words, conveys vocal expression and can also have an impact on how well you are understood—from a mechanical point of view—especially on the phone.

Excited or anxious people often speak quickly. The listener becomes confused from too much information coming too rapidly and because the words are often garbled and indistinct. If you speak too quickly you will often be made aware of it. Your listener will ask you to repeat what you have said, or even say "Slow down a minute!" If that happens, stop, take a deep breath, relax, and start again.

59

Not Too Fast . . .

On the other hand, a slow rate of speech may convey tiredness, uncertainty, lack of interest and lack of confidence. Slow speech can be a challenge, especially on the phone when your physical presence cannot help you hold your audience. People become impatient with slow speakers (unless they speak slowly themselves) and their attention wanders.

Some people mistakenly believe that it is necessary to speak more slowly than normal on the phone to ensure being heard. Not so. Slowing down will not improve understanding. The phone does not hinder hearing or distort the thinking process. People do not need more time to understand what they hear over the phone. Speaking slowly will not improve understanding. It will discourage interest. Use an ordinary, conversational rate of speech. A good way to determine whether your rate of speech is right is to invite reactions from your listener.

When Slowness Helps

There are times when speaking slowly is necessary, such as when spelling out names or numbers, or giving a message that you wish to be written down exactly. A good rule of thumb is to match the rate of the person you are talking with. People are more comfortable listening to the rate with which they speak.

Speak slowly when talking with angry people. Anger makes people speak quickly. If you respond at the same rate, you may increase the anger. Speaking slowly yourself can be the first step in calming the anger. Remember this when you deal with the complaints you may receive. Speaking slowly suggests calmness, and that is contagious.

Volume

Volume is loudness or softness of your voice. Do not confuse it with *pitch.* You do not need to increase your volume to be heard because the phone transmitter does the work for you. Also, since you are speaking into a mouthpiece inches from your mouth and the listener is receiving your words in a receiver held to her or his ear, you are closer than you would be in a face-to-face conversation.

You probably have had the experience of having to move the receiver away from your ear in order to avoid a blast of sound. Or perhaps you have heard someone's voice coming through loud and clear—on someone else's phone. A too-loud voice is annoying and even painful. Become aware of the volume of your voice. A good way to do this is to record yourself using a tape recorder when you are talking to a friend on the telephone.

60

While you will avoid shouting or talking too loudly over the phone, you will also want to avoid the other extreme of talking too softly. To be sure you are understood, speak in a normal volume with the mouthpiece two or three inches from your lips.

Using Volume
You will want to use volume to express emotions occasionally when appropriate. You increase volume to express emotions such as anger, amusement, excitement, confidence, surprise, pain. Most people lower their volume to express sorrow, tiredness, secretiveness.

Do so when talking on the phone, but to a lesser degree—do not raise your voice as high, nor lower it as low as you might in a face-to-face conversation. If you do need to say something loudly, move the mouthpiece away from your lips. Take a tip from the professional singers you see on television. They hold the microphone within two or three inches of their lips most of the time, but when they raise the volume of their voice they move the microphone further away.

Your voice volume can be loud, moderate, or quiet. Most of the time, moderate volume is best. A variety of factors can affect your volume just as they can affect your pitch. Most of the factors affecting volume are within your control, and if you are aware of them, you can avoid having them cause your volume to become unsuitable for the message you are conveying.

Tension and Volume
As it does pitch, tension affects volume. When people are tense or nervous, their throat muscles tighten, and their volume becomes uncomfortable and unnatural. You may have seen suspense movies in which an individual becomes too scared to make any sound at all or perhaps can only whimper. Or there are scenes in which a frightened person screams. These represent extreme situations, but they can happen when a person's throat muscles become tight from tension.

Tension can cause you to speak loudly or to be barely able to talk. Tension has many causes. You want to recognize what might cause tension for you and try to reduce or eliminate the causes. When feeling tense, concentrate on maintaining moderate volume. Use the tension-reducing techniques you will read of in Chapter Eight to help you maintain a moderate voice volume.

Energy and Volume

Your level of energy and enthusiasm will affect your volume. If you are not feeling well, or have little energy or enthusiasm, the volume of your voice will be low (also your rate of speech will be slower). If you are rested and enjoy your work, your voice will usually have a pleasant, moderate volume.

Controlling Volume

Your mouth size and speech habits can affect volume. Men usually have greater volume than women because they have larger mouths. You can not change your mouth size, of course, but you can use your mouth to change your volume.

For example, some people have developed the habit of speaking without moving their jaw much. They have a closed-mouth manner of speaking; they speak through their teeth. This produces unclear sounds and low volume that makes it difficult for listeners on phones to understand what is being said.

Avoid the opposite extreme as well. You know that when you want to give a big yell, you open your mouth wide. Some people open their mouths wide and expel a lot of air when talking on the phone. This produces an unwelcome loudness.

Do not talk through your teeth nor open your mouth as if to yell when on the phone. Move your jaw and open your mouth sufficiently to say the words clearly at a moderate volume.

Judging Volume

Judging your own volume is difficult to do. You know when you are whispering, of course, and when you are shouting. At least, you think you do and you do to some extent. The problem is that the way our voices sound in our own ears can be quite different from how they sound to others. Further, as noted earlier, what is normal volume for some people may seem like shouting to others. Work with your classmates, friends, and others, to try to determine how you sound and what your volume is.

As with rate of speech, you must be particularly careful to control your volume when you are talking with someone who is upset and shouting. The human tendency is to reply in kind. Do not get into shouting matches. A quiet voice suggests calmness and reason and that will help lessen the other's anger.

Emphasis

You create **emphasis** by raising or lowering your voice—either volume or pitch—or pausing as you speak. Raising or lowering your voice is known as **inflection**. Doing so—using inflection—makes your voice expressive and varied. Without inflection, your voice is a **monotone**, which means you speak at the same, unvaried level. You use just one note, which lacks expression and emphasis.

Emphasis—inflection and pauses—serves in spoken sentences much as punctuation marks do in written sentences. Actually, considering that speaking came before writing, it is more appropriate to say punctuation marks are used in written sentences for the emphasis we can convey with our spoken voice or with our body.

Body language can be used to emphasize your spoken word in face-to-face conversation. On the telephone you have only your voice to do the job. Along with pauses and inflection, you also have volume and rate of speech to help you add emphasis to your telephone voice.

Inflections Convey Meaning

In addition to providing emphasis, upward and downward inflections convey different meanings. One way we know that a sentence is a question is that the speaker raises his or her voice at the end. Perhaps you know someone who always ends a sentence this way. It probably sounds to you as if that person is always a bit unsure.

Ending phrases or sentences with downward inflection makes you sound knowledgeable and decisive, because the sentence does not seem to be a question. To test how upward and downward inflection can change meaning, try saying the following simple sentence with different inflections.

■ This is great

Upward inflection puts a question mark at the end. The speaker is questioning its greatness. Downward inflection puts a period at the end. The speaker is asserting its greatness.

Inflections and Monotones

Sometimes upward and downward inflections are heard in the same word or sentence. These mixed inflections add life to speech. We convey much meaning with the use of emphasis: conviction, uncertainty, sor-

Even if your pronunciation and articulation are perfect, what you say may not be the same as what your listener hears. Not only the sound of your speech, but the words you choose as well have an effect. Guard against assuming that everybody understands a word in the same way you do.

We all interpret words differently, depending on our experience and perspective. To minimize misunderstanding, keep these things in mind as you decide what to say:

✔ Be specific. Replace less specific words like "old" or "large" with more detailed information. For example, an "old house" in New England might be 200-250 years old, while in San Francisco, a house is considered old if it is 150 years old. A better phrase would be "a house built in 1825."

✔ Avoid jargon. As you get to know your company and its business well, you will learn the technical and specialized language used there. Be careful not to let it creep into your conversations with people who may not have the same familiarity with it that you do.

✔ If you do have to use technical language, avoid talking down to your listener. Explain the terms you use, but don't make the other person feel stupid for not knowing them. Explain them in a matter-of-fact tone, as though it is standard procedure—which it should be—and not a comment on that individual's knowledge.

✔ Avoid cliches, slang, worn-out words. Words fall into and out of fashion. Sixties words and phrases like "groovy" or "doing my own thing" have been replaced today by "radical" and "totally." Try to find words and phrases that will not be dated in a few weeks or years.

✔ Watch for aggressive words and phrases. Phrases like "tell you," "talk to you," "you should," "demand," "want," and others, have an aggressive feel, implying that your listener is not worthy of your consideration. A switch to "describe for you," "talk with you," "would you consider" creates a more considerate and nonaggressive tone.

63

row, joy. We expect to hear emphasis when people speak. We find a monotone—a complete lack of emphasis—boring.

If you have a tendency to speak in a monotone, listen to others to develop an awareness of how inflections add color and life to speech. Although largely an automatic response, you can develop your use of emphasis with practice.

Eliminating Interference

None of what you have read in this chapter will help you speak effectively on the phone if your phone does not transmit your voice clearly or other factors interfere. If it is not broken, your phone will transmit clearly as long as you do not do things that interfere with it.

The rule, "Don't talk with your mouth full." is particularly important when you are on the phone. Do not eat, drink, smoke, or chew gum. If you must eat while on duty, clear your mouth before answering the phone. Restrict smoking and gum chewing to break time.

To the extent you have control, minimize background noise. Offices are busy and sometimes noisy places, with machines running, people talking, and phones ringing. You cannot do much about that. But you can stop any background noises you might be producing.

These include tapping your pen or pencil on the desk or the phone itself, fluttering papers noisily, snapping elastic bands, and so forth. Be aware of any habits like these you may have developed—and try to break them. Such noises distract your listeners.

Hold Your Phone Correctly

Hold your phone properly. Keep the mouthpiece two or three inches from your mouth. Make sure it is not tucked under your chin or touching your mouth, because these change the sound of your voice. Avoid holding the phone against your ear with your shoulder as this will cause your voice to become muffled and indistinct.

Take Care of Your Voice

Here are some ways for taking care of your voice so that you can use it effectively without straining.

✓ Do warm-up exercises for a few moments before beginning a day of talking on the phone. Hum the musical scale (do, re, mi) with your mouth closed, then open, slowly and quietly at first, gradually faster and louder. Move your voice up as many octaves as you can.

✓ Make sure you can breathe easily. Sit or stand up straight. Wear clothes that are not so tight they restrict your breathing.

✓ Speak from your diaphragm. When you breathe you can feel your diaphragm rising and falling beneath your rib cage. When you speak, push air out from deep inside—you do not have to speak loudly to do this.

✓ Do not use your voice when you have a cold or a cough. Not only will you not be able to speak clearly, you will be interrupted with coughs and talking will strain your voice. Talking on the phone is particularly irritating to sore throats.

✓ Avoid foods and beverages that can adversely affect your voice when you know you will be using the phone. Chocolate and milk products, for example, increase mucus production that can make it necessary for you to clear your throat when talking. Alcohol and cigarettes irritate your throat and can change the sound of your voice, making it raspy and harsh.

✓ Avoid smokey or extra dry air, which can impair your voice and make speaking difficult.

Quiz Questions

1. Define *correct pronunciation* and *good articulation.*

2. People are accustomed to occasional mispronunciations and are not distracted by them. Do you agree? Explain your answer.

3. How does tension affect articulation?

4. Name some good personal habits that will lead to good articulation.

5. Why is the tone of your voice so important?

6. How does having a smile on your face affect your conversation on the telephone?

7. What kind of change in pitch will benefit most speakers? Give examples.

8. Generally it is not necessary to speak slowly over the phone to be understood. However, cite two times when slower speech may be helpful.

9. What is inflection and how does it help your conversation?

10. Describe how to hold a phone properly.

Discussion Questions

1. List five tips for pronouncing words correctly and give examples.

2. Describe briefly how each characteristic of your voice affects how you sound to your listeners.

3. Cite five rules for taking care of your voice.

Activities

1. With a classmate tape a 15-minute conversation. Talk on unfamiliar topics using unfamiliar words. Use a formal tone that you might use at work. Replay the tape. Stop the tape as needed to discuss pronunciation, articulation, tone, pitch, volume, rate, and emphasis. List improvements you can make, even if they are as simple as not saying "um" often.

2. Select a two– or three–paragraph passage from this textbook, a newspaper, or any book. Read it into a tape recorder in a normal voice. Re-read it a few times, making these changes: speak loudly for one paragraph then softly for another; read one sarcastically, one humorously, one sadly; change emphasis, exaggerate one paragraph, read one in a monotone; change pitch from high for one to low for another; read one quickly, one slowly.
Play back the tape and note how the changes sound. Compare them to the sound of your normal voice. Note when the changes make it difficult for you to understand what you said. Find a friend or family member to listen to the tape. Have your listener tell you when the changes adversely affected how clearly you spoke.

3. Find a classmate to be a partner; make an appointment to call your partner. Each should have something to eat and drink, papers to shuffle, a pen to click, a pencil to tap. During the telephone conversation, make extraneous noise and talk while eating or drinking. Do not overdo it. The point is to get a realistic experience. When eating or drinking, try to conceal it, as you might if doing it on the job; when clicking a pen, do not hold it next to the phone, but at a natural distance. Listen to the effect of the noise on the voice coming over the phone. While this activity may end up seeming humorous, imagine the effect on a customer.

Chapter Six

Preparing for Business Calls

Upon completing this chapter you will be able to:

① *recognize how knowing your company's products and services improves call handling,*

② *identify where in your company you can turn for information,*

③ *plan what to say on the telephone.*

In previous chapters you read about the importance of listening and speaking skills, and of notetaking and understanding how to use phone equipment. All these skills will be of little use in handling calls without thorough knowledge of your company.

The more you know about your company's products and services, the more credibility you will project, and the more confident you will feel. You will be able to provide accurate information, refer people quickly and efficiently to the correct department, and generally be able to distinguish between calls that are important or unimportant to the company. You will be able to extend yourself for your company's customers or clients, which is an important part of building solid business relationships.

To develop your knowledge about your business you will first of all need to learn what you know and do not know. Next you will need to find how to get the information you require. Once you have the information, you will want to put it to use. This chapter will show you ways of getting to know your company.

Know What You Know

When you first take a job, it is hard to gauge what you know and do not know. There is so much to learn: how to find your way around the office building, the names of your coworkers, where to find supplies, learning about company benefits and office procedures.

On top of all that, you need to learn about the business and its products or services. You also need to know something about the general category of business that your company is in. Below are three major categories of business and a little about each. Your company might or might not fit into one of these categories.

Professional practices, such as law, medicine, engineering. Many employees in these professions have advanced degrees. In recognition of this when writing their name they often use abbreviations such as M.D. (for medical doctor), Esq. (for esquire, used by lawyers), P.E. (for professional engineer).

Trades include businesses such as construction, lawn care, electrical work. Many employees in these businesses are trained in technical skills, such as plumbing, tree surgery, electrical wiring. They may be licensed or certified by a government agency or trade association.

Manufacturing companies produce products for sale to other companies. For example, steel manufacturers produce steel for the automotive industry to use in making cars. Printers manufacture books for publishing companies who sell the books to bookstores.

Your field of work may have a specialized language that you will have to learn. There may be specially designed computer software that you will be trained to use. You will need to learn company **policies** that govern how business is conducted. You might need to learn the policies for making payments, offering discounts, accepting returned items, offering warrantees, offering credit.

Anyone starting a new job can expect to feel overwhelmed by all the new things to learn. You may talk to customers on the phone who do not realize you have been with the firm only a few days. Good phone techniques will help you during this time.

Use Your Training

Most companies have orientation and training programs for new employees. In-service training is increasingly a feature of business careers. In large companies, this training period may be up to two or more weeks in length and be highly structured with lectures, films, demonstrations, and employee handbooks to read.

Even very small companies will make sure you spend a few days to a week with someone who can train you for the job. Perhaps it will be the person you are replacing. No matter what your training period is like, make sure you take full advantage of it. Here are some ways.

✓ Take notes. You will not be able to remember everything unaided. Organize them, indexing if necessary, so that you can find the information again.

✓ Concentrate. Remember where to go for information rather than trying to absorb all the details in the beginning.

✓ Ask questions. When you are new at your job, no one expects you to know all that you need to know. It is better to ask your questions in the beginning rather than after being on the job several months. You need not worry about not seeming knowledgeable when you are learning.

69

Add to Your Expertise

Your initial training will give you the basics. You could decide that you now know all you need to get by. But your work will be more interesting if you continue to explore and you will be more valuable to your company, which increases your opportunities for advancement. To grow and become more knowledgeable in your job, you will have to do some personal outreach.

You may wonder at times why you had to learn some things—especially things you never actively use or will not use for a long time. Almost always, however, the more you know, the more you see how things are interconnected and affect one another—how your job fits in.

An efficient receptionist in a dentist's office knows how long various procedures take. A routine cleaning is done in a short time while root canal work takes much longer. This helps the receptionist avoid scheduling appointments too closely, causing patients annoying waits. Here are ways to add to your knowledge.

✓ Develop a healthy curiosity about your company and its products or services. Talk to long-time workers, to people who work in other departments. You will gain useful background information. Seek useful information. Avoid gossip.

✓ Develop a list of resource people with the kinds of information you might need to do your job.

✓ Read company announcements about personnel changes and new products or services. Check the bulletin board regularly.

✓ Learn to use procedures manuals, reports, catalogs, and files.

✓ Read trade magazines and other publications in your field.

✓ Take advantage of in-service training. After you have been with the company for a while you may be eligible for tuition credits or to attend adult education courses, conferences, seminars, and lectures pertinent to your field in general and your job in particular.

Admit Your Lack of Knowledge

Perhaps you have heard this before: "It's better to ask a dumb question than to make a dumb mistake." Actually no question is a dumb question. Do not consider how you or your question will appear; the important thing is for you to find out what you need to know.

You will learn what you do not know in a variety of ways. You will hear coworkers talking and realize you are not familiar with what they are discussing. A customer will ask you a question that you cannot answer. You will be given an assignment that you find difficult.

Follow up on these right away. Faking it—pretending you know when you actually do not know—will get you into trouble later. Admit your lack of knowledge. Get the answers. Try never to be unable to answer the same question twice. Ask for a refresher on procedures or details you feel unsure about. Ask to be taught things you find you need to know but for which you have not been trained.

71

Know How to Find Out

While there is value in knowing a great deal about your company, it is neither necessary nor possible to know it all. What is important is knowing where to turn for information so you can transfer calls to the right department, or be able to assure your customers confidently that you can get information for them and call right back.

Before going on, here is a reminder about phone techniques. When you are new in a company you will want to introduce yourself to other employees and clients. Here are some possible opening phrases to use.

> *Good morning, Mrs. Bartels. I am (name). I've recently joined the company as the replacement for (name).*

> *Good morning, Mr. Yoshi. I am your new customer service representative at (Company).*

> *Good morning, Ms. Pinella. I am calling in response to your letter to Bill Hastings. As you may know, Bill is no long with (Company). I have taken over his responsibilities.*

> *Good morning, Mr. Archer. I have just joined (Company) as the marketing assistant for (name).*

Organization Chart

An **organization chart** shows how a company is organized into various groups by function. It also indicates a written or unwritten order of decision making, reporting, communication, and specialization of activity. Your company may have a printed organization chart or you can draw one for yourself as you learn about the company.

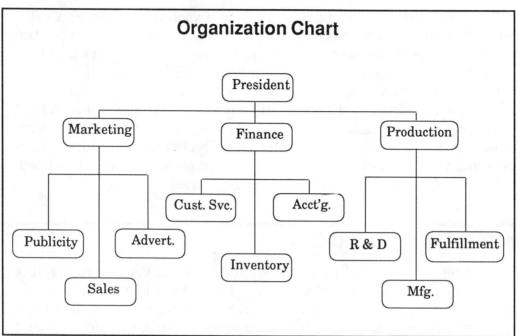

Organization Chart

Organization charts demonstrate the relationships among various departments within a company. Besides showing who reports to whom, they help visualize how tasks are dealt with and how responsibilities are assigned.

72

See the example of an organizational chart above. It shows a company divided into three functional groups—marketing, finance, and production. It also shows the subdivisions within the three groups. Here are some other things you can learn from the chart.

✓ Customer service is in the financial group, not marketing where you might expect it to be.

✓ Suppose you are not certain whether the publicity manager or the advertising manager has certain information you need. You could ask the marketing manager, who overseas both advertising and publicity.

✓ You will see that Research and Development (commonly referred to as R & D) is carried out in the production group. In another company this might be a separate department, even reporting directly to the President.

Many organization charts also give names of individuals in key positions. An organization chart will not do you much good until you understand what each section represents and what activities are carried out there. You will want to answer questions such as the following:

✓ What activities are done in the Marketing Department, and how does that affect my job?

✓ Are the heads of marketing, finance, and production vice presidents of the company? If so, do they like to have their titles used when they are being referred to?

✓ If someone asks me a question about a product warranty, what department do I refer them to?

73

✓ Is there a Personnel Department in the company and in which section does it belong?

As you discover the answers to these kinds of questions, make a note with the phone number or extension on your organizational chart, which you can then use as a quick reference sheet. Earlier we suggested developing a list of resource people who can help you. This information can be added to the chart as well.

Mini-Reference Library

Chances are your company or business prepares and distributes to customers and employees all kinds of printed material, such as brochures, product catalogs, annual reports, product specification sheets, and policy and procedure manuals. Collect these in your own personal mini-reference library, and read through to become familiar with what they contain, then file them for easy reference near your desk and phone.

Obviously, not all will be directly pertinent to your everyday needs. But, like the in-depth knowledge we discussed earlier, having access to this information will pay off in the long run.

After you have been working with the company for a while, you may have to sort through your mini-reference library and discard out-dated materials. Organize other material into files such as for "this year's model" and "last year's model" or files for a specific product line by name. Create files for information that you receive regularly, such as production schedules or price changes.

Try to keep your library well organized and up-to-date. If it is difficult to use or merely adds to clutter on your desk, you will not wish, or be able, to refer to it. Weed out old material that is no longer accurate or that you have memorized.

Knowledge Helps Planning

Planning what you are going to say on the phone is important. Your knowledge of the company will help you to plan the purpose of a call. Anticipate the needs and possible questions of the person you are calling. Use your knowledge of the company to get answers and information in advance.

Gather Information In Advance

74

Suppose the purpose of your call is to obtain information. Perhaps there is information you can provide first that will help the other person give you the information you need. For example, you are helping arrange your company's exhibit at an upcoming trade show. You need to find out the hours for setting up the booth. Before making your call to the convention bureau, ask yourself what the convention bureau might ask you. They might ask if you need help in moving heavy equipment because, if so, it would affect how they answer your question. With this information in front of you when you call you will not have to hunt for it while on the phone.

Jim McMullen's doctor took a blood sample and sent it to Penn Medical Laboratories for analysis. Shortly after he returned home, Jim's phone rang and someone said, "Mr. McMullen? This is Sheila at Penn Labs. We have a sample of your blood here. Could you tell me your birth date?" Jim gave the date, the technician said "Thank you" and hung up.

A few moments later, he got another call: "Mr. McMullen, this is Mrs. Johnson at Penn Labs. Could you give me your insurance policy number for your lab work?" Jim supplied the number. Mrs. Johnson said "Thank you" and hung up. Within moments, the phone rang again, "Mr. McMullen? This is Sheila at Penn Labs. I'm sorry to bother you again, but do you spell your name McMullen or MacMullen?"

As far as Jim McMullen could tell from his experience with Penn Labs, the people who worked there were pleasant, but he knew they had not planned what to say on the phone carefully. He might conclude that at Penn Labs one hand does not know what the other hand is doing.

Be aware of changes in your company that will be of interest to the person you are calling. For example, suppose you have to call a person who has been dealing with a customer service representative a long time. You recently saw a personnel announcement saying this representative has retired. Plan ahead and find out who now handles that person's account. If the customer asks you what happened to the representative, you can give an informed response.

A broad and thorough base of information increases your ability to field questions and get results on the phone.

Develop a List of Questions

75

If your phone work requires you to obtain information from customers and clients, then consider developing a basic list of questions, which you can write down and refer to until they become second nature. The purpose of the basic list is to ensure that you ask all the necessary questions before you hang up. You do not have to ask the questions in sequence and sometimes you may omit some of the questions. You may have to develop more than one list to meet varied needs.

As we see from the experience of Jim McMullen (see the box on page 74), Penn Lab's employees could have demonstrated better professional telephone skills. If Sheila had made a list of questions to ask Jim she might not have had to call twice. If she and Mrs. Johnson knew more about each other's jobs they might have agreed that one of them could get all the information in just one call. (See the box on page 76.)

Balance Your Approach

When making many calls of a similar nature, you can sound as if you are speaking by **rote**, that is, as if you are reciting from memory rather than talking with someone. After a while that may indeed be the case. You may be efficient but you will not sound interesting or lively. Therefore, you will want to balance your basic approach with several variations.

To create variety, use your imagination. A dictionary or thesaurus will provide you with new words or synonyms (words that have the same meaning), for just about any word you have to use. In addition to selecting new words, you may also want to reorganize phrases, change inflections and emphasis. If your company sells a variety of products or services you will have more variety in what you say. If only one product is offered, try to find different ways to describe it.

When you want to remember what you need to say during phone conversations, but do not have a script, a checklist can be a handy memory-jog for the important points you need to cover. Checklists can be especially useful when you need to ask the other person questions.

The list below covers questions you would ask in many situations, whatever business you are in. It makes sure you pick up the essential information for doing business. The points may seem obvious, but the whole reason for having a checklist is that it is very easy to forget what seems obvious in the abstract when you are in the middle of an actual call.

Other questions would depend on the business and the reason for your call. If you were placing a sales call you might need information about what the person currently owns, about finances, or about the size of the business. If you were arranging an appointment for a face-to-face meeting, you would put asking for directions on your checklist—and so on.

- ✔ First name (with correct spelling and pronunciation)
- ✔ Last name (with correct spelling and pronunciation)
- ✔ Middle initial
- ✔ Date of birth
- ✔ Address (include floor, department, office, apartment, or other relevant items)
- ✔ Phone number (include extension where applicable)
- ✔ Occupation or title
- ✔ Invoice or PO number (if for a sales-related call)
- ✔ Date of purchase (if for a sales-related call)

In some businesses, especially telemarketing or product sales via the telephone, employees use a prepared **telephone dialog** . This is more elaborate than a basic question list. It may include opening remarks, a description of products or services, a benefit statement, and fact-finding questions. Usually the statements and questions in the telephone dialog are read in the same sequence each time. Employees are given a telephone dialog or make up their own. Using a prepared telephone dialog is the most efficient way to handle this kind of call.

Quiz Questions

1. List three reasons why knowing your company's products and services improves call handling.

2. What does company policy refer to and what are some examples of specific company policies?

3. List the hints described in the text to help you take full advantage of your training period.

4. When you are new to the company, are there special ways you might want to introduce yourself to other employees and clients?

5. Describe how to add to your knowledge after training.

6. Pretending you know something you actually do not know gets you into trouble. What should you do instead?

7. Give several examples of places you can turn to for information about your company.

8. What shows you how a company is organized?

9. What are three things you can do to plan what to say on the phone?

10. What is the purpose of a basic question list?

Discussion Questions

1. Discuss features you might expect of an initial training program. Describe training experiences, good and bad, which you have had for summer or part-time jobs. Did any of the training cover professional telephone skills?

2. Explain the value of learning more about the business or service than you might ever actually use.

Activities

1. Join with at least two other students to describe experiences you all have had on the phone. Try to remember personal business calls—to the phone company, a doctor's office, or a local store—when the person on the phone did not have thorough company knowledge. How did that affect that person's ability to help you? Make a list of the rec-

ommendations on how the person with whom you spoke can improve his or her knowledge and performance.

2. Practice varying your words. Write down at least five ways to say each of the following sentences or phrases:

- ■ *Please tell me your name?*
- ■ *beautiful old house*
- ■ *modern software package*
- ■ *Good morning, (your name) of Mutual Insurance Company. May I help you?*
- ■ *How do you pronounce your name, please?*
- ■ *Is this a good time to talk?*
- ■ *good service*

78

Chapter Seven

Projecting a Positive Image

Upon completing this chapter you will be able to:

① *maintain professional objectivity,*

② *project positive control with a three-step process,*

③ *employ assertiveness and positive language to counter negative attitudes,*

④ *use a self-questioning technique to maintain a positive attitude.*

In previous chapters you learned some basic professional telephone skills. Using these will help you project a professional image on the phone. Another part—an important part—of a professional bearing is having a positive attitude and that has to come from within you—from your conscious and unconscious attitudes. As with the mechanical skills, however, you can learn and develop habits that will help you maintain and project a positive attitude. In this chapter you will read about the importance of attitude when using the telephone and of strategies for maintaining a positive attitude.

Your thoughts, emotions, and feelings—even those you may not be actively aware of—affect your attitude and your manner. Positive thoughts and feelings generate positive attitudes. Negative thoughts generate negative attitudes. And your attitude will affect your communication. You can control negative thoughts, reject them, and maintain positive thoughts that will lead to a positive disposition.

Positive attitude does not mean the superficial mouthing of "Have a nice day" prevalent in all kinds of businesses from banks to fast-food outlets. A positive attitude includes having and using positive interpersonal skills that actually create a nice day for people you deal with.

Stress can generate negative thoughts and attitudes. You will read in Chapter Eight of ways to control and reduce stress. This chapter will focus on general strategies for reducing negative and encouraging positive thoughts and attitudes.

A large part of your success in life depends on your attitude. As the saying has it, "It's not so much what happens to you that matters, but how you react."

Keeping a Professional Objectivity

It is impossible to avoid all negative thoughts and moods. It is normal to experience, now and then, the urge to speak sharply or to hang up on a caller who is giving you a hard time. Do not make the mistake of thinking that if you ignore them, your negative thoughts will not affect your attitude. They will. Do not ignore your negative thoughts. Change them to positive ones. The key to keeping a professional objectivity is controlling and changing negative thoughts and resisting the urge to act on them. To do this, you must first accept the fact that you will have them. Thus prepared, you can more readily shake them off rather than act on them. How you act often determines how you feel, as well as the other way round. If you act positively you will begin to feel that way, even if it is an effort at first.

It is important to be able to defuse initial feelings of being upset without speaking out and without building up a sense of resentment. Even if you do not do anything deliberately rude, for example, your behavior—tone of voice, rate of speech, and so forth—often reflects any annoyance that you, unconsciously or otherwise, harbor. Even in saying such a harmless, conventional phrase, as "Good Morning," you will project your mood unless you are careful. And if you are unaware of any lingering resentment, you may well not be careful.

Attitudes are Catching

Attitudes can be caught just as you catch a cold, which is another reason why you must be on guard. If people around you are laughing, your inclination is to laugh also. If you have an exchange with a negative person, your inclination is to be negative.

Imagine that you have just come to work. The first few telephone calls and conversations with coworkers go smoothly. Then you get a customer on the line with a complaint. Nothing you say satisfies this person; you can feel your heart racing and you rack your brain trying to think of something to say to soothe the customer.

The exchange goes poorly. The customer hangs up abruptly, unsatisfied. The phone rings again. This time it is a customer with a simple inquiry but, still thinking of that last exchange, instead of your usual helpful tone you say testily, "Yes, what is it?" The customer responds defensively, wondering what it was he or she did to justify your tone. He or she also probably thinks, "I don't need this kind of treatment; I'll take my business elsewhere."

Unless you take action to change it, your negative mood will continue to spread both inside and outside of the business, perhaps even be taken home to family members. The negative attitude can come from a colleague, customer, or client, affecting and infecting you and everyone that you come in contact with.

Subtle Negative Messages

Negative attitudes can have less obvious, but nonetheless undesirable, results. For example, you send subtle negative messages when you treat callers mechanically, hardly giving them any time and putting off their requests. Not returning phone calls is another example of subtle negative behavior. There are often *excuses* for this behavior: deadlines, many interruptions, or a flood of requests that make you want to cut a call short. There are few good *reasons*.

Although this kind of behavior is not actually impolite, it is definitely a sign of a negative attitude. With subtle discouragement, the caller just goes away and leaves the worker alone. Employees who get into the habit of discouraging callers put their company at risk of losing business and themselves at risk of being fired.

82

Taking Charge

You are subjected to positive or negative thoughts and attitudes all day long—knowingly and unknowingly. You can take charge and screen your own negative thoughts, such as "That person was really rude to me." "I'm so tired." "I won't take that kind of treatment again." and replace them with positive ones.

To help yourself suppress negative thoughts and the impulse to reply in kind when dealing with a rude or upset person, keep in mind that in most business situations, you, personally, are not the target. The ire is not directed at you as an individual. It has really nothing to do with you. Remaining aware of this will help you limit your own annoyance without building up a reservoir of resentment.

Maintaining positive thoughts can be a challenge when encountering negative expressions and actions. Making an effort does help, however. When you catch yourself framing negative thoughts, try to turn them into positive ones. Positive thoughts stimulate positive physical and mental reactions that yield positive results.

Consider this three-step process to take charge of negative thoughts.

1. Be aware of negative moods so as to be able to change them immediately.

2. Generate positive thoughts and concentrate on them.

3. After concentrating on a positive thought for one or two minutes, go back to your productive work and you will be amazed at your change in attitude.

Often, negative thoughts are so strong that it is hard to think of anything positive. Try to prepare ideas in advance that you can concentrate on when this occurs.

Two Tools

When others are negative you have two powerful tools at your disposal to counter their negative attitude and help you take charge of the mood. These are assertiveness and positive language.

Assertiveness

Suppose you find yourself at the receiving end of a subtle put-off. You have placed a call requesting additional information from your insurance agent on a policy you have purchased. The answer you get is "All health insurance policies are worded that way." or "We've never had anyone ask that before and its never been a problem." or "Don't worry, I'm sure it's fine."

83

You probably would feel that your agent is unhelpful and putting you off. You could take your business elsewhere, ask to speak to the boss, get angry, or be *assertive*. Being **assertive** is being firm, fair, and friendly. It does not mean to be pushy and insisting on having things done your way. In this example, when your agent realizes that you will not fade away, you will get results.

To be firm, you need to show that you will be persistent. You can do that by repeating your request, perhaps rephrasing it slightly, as often as necessary to make your point and to get some action. Repeat responses to your request so the speaker understands that you heard what he or she said. This also makes nonanswers obvious. Show you are fair by telling the speaker that you understand the situation, but you feel entitled to an answer; that you appreciate the effort he or she makes to help you. Use a friendly tone of voice. This approach is the most positive you can use.

Using Positive Language

The language you use can create negative impressions without your being aware of it. Consider these examples of negative language and their positive counterparts:

✓ Weather forecasters describe sunny weather as "nice" and rainy weather as

Being firm and friendly is an effective approach on the telephone. You can assert yourself with a smile and positive language.

"bad" even when we need rain.

✓ A supplier might say, "We can't get it until next week," when "We can get it as early as next week" would do as well.

✓ A credit officer might say "You can't get credit with an account under $2,000." The same person could say, "You will be eligible for credit as soon as your account reaches $2,000."

84

If you find other people are being negative, you can change the tone of the conversation by using positive language. You do not have to argue or agree with them, try to change their minds, or cheer them up. Just take charge by acknowledging the other's statement "I understand what you mean," and moving on positively, "How can I help you?"

To keep the conversation upbeat, choose positive phrasing whenever you can. For example, instead of "What's the matter?" say "Please tell me about the circumstances."

If you are having difficulty understanding the other person, do not say "I don't know what you are talking about," instead try "Could you please explain that again?"

If you have to refuse a request or answer negatively, try not to leave the person flat; express regret and offer alternatives—for example, instead of "That is out of stock until next week," say "We will have that for you as soon as next week."

A positive image is not something you flash briefly now and then. If you have put customers off or been unhelpful, you cannot undo the damage by chirping, "Have a nice day!" at the end of the conversation. You must work to maintain a positive image that will be reflected from your opening "Hello" to your final "Good-bye."

Attitudes from Within

Outside events play a large part in setting your mood at any particularly time, but another important factor influencing your moods comes from within. Your own sense of yourself and what you expect to happen will influence your attitudes. If you maintain a poor self-image, you will have a doubtful, hopeless attitude toward whatever you try to accomplish and expect the worst. Such an attitude affects your behavior and, ultimately, the results you do realize.

Imagine someone with a poor self-image preparing to make a phone call to seek a job interview. "This is a waste of time, I'm not going to get this job," the caller thinks. To avoid anticipated disappointment, the caller assumes an "I don't really care if I get this job" tone while speaking to the prospective employer. The employer hears this tone and decides that a more interested and upbeat employee is preferable. The employer discourages the caller. The caller hangs up thinking, "I *knew* that this would be a waste of time."

This illustrates what is known as the **self-fulfilling prophecy**, which means that what you expect to happen happens, because you expect it and act in a way to bring it about. In effect, your subconscious mind believes what you tell it. Your subconscious mind influences your attitude and, consequently, colors your actions. The result will most likely be what you anticipate.

Fortunately, the self-fulfilling prophecy works the same way with positive thoughts. If you have positive thoughts, the chances for positive results increase. Before making the call in the example above, if the person had prepared with positive thoughts predicting a positive outcome, the job interview would probably have been granted.

85

Looking Within

To change your own negativity, identify its causes and devise ways for dealing with them. It may be difficult to recognize your own attitudes. One way is by **introspection**—by looking inside yourself, by thinking about how you approach life and work and asking yourself questions.

Here are some examples of questions you can ask yourself. The answers will suggest—only suggest—a positive or negative pattern of thinking. Think about them and answer each as honestly as you can.

1. (a) Do I tend to put off tasks? (b) Do I make every effort to do the task at hand rather than put it off?

2. (a) Do I feel threatened and insecure when I do not know the answer to a question someone asks me? (b) Do I feel challenged to find the answer?

3. (a) Do I limit myself to the easiest way of doing something? (b) Am I willing to explore new, challenging endeavors?

4. (a) Do I find that my mood is easily affected by everything from the weather to how others treat me? (b) Can I function effectively regardless of circumstances?

5. (a) Is my work area cluttered and my time so fragmented that I am unable to complete tasks on time? (b) Do I keep my work area orderly and my time well managed so that I am able to do what needs to be done?

A "yes" answer to more than two of the (a) questions indicates a negative pattern of avoidance and resistance rather than a positive pattern of motivation and initiative.

There may be reasons for developing negative patterns. Sometimes people find themselves in the wrong career. Perhaps they are trying to satisfy another's expectations or they have misjudged their interest in a field. Over time they lose their commitment to succeed, and merely put time in at the job, expending the least possible effort. Sometimes people adopt negative patterns when their knowledge and training do not fit the requirements of the job. Handicapped by lack of information or experience, their self-confidence is diminished.

86

Overcoming Negative Patterns

Fortunately, growth and change are possible. Recognize negative patterns as symptoms of challenges to meet instead of hopeless traps. For some people, a change in career or additional training or schooling is what is needed to break a pattern of avoidance and resistance. Most of the time the challenge is smaller and more easily solved. Here are some positive approaches to the situations posed in the questions above:

1. *Do I tend to put off tasks?* Look for a pattern in your behavior. Each time you think, "Oh, well, I can do that later," see if it is always about the same task. Perhaps you avoid doing it because you fear you cannot do it or you will make a mistake. Remember the self-fulfilling prophecy. Tell yourself you can do it and try. Anticipation is usually worse than reality. Perhaps you procrastinate when you dislike a task or find it boring or too big. Break it into smaller pieces. Do a little of it, alternate doing something you dislike with doing something you enjoy. Continue until the task is done.

2. *Do I feel threatened and insecure when I do not know the answer?* When your knowledge is thin, you may avoid responding to inquiries or find yourself defensive when challenged. Take action, be assertive. Learn as much as you can so that you can confidently project a positive image. Never be afraid to admit a lack of knowledge. Face it and ask questions.

3. *Do I limit myself to the easiest way of doing something?* The key to this one is the words "I can." Self-limiting peo-

ple often say "I can't." What they mean is "I don't really want to." If you find yourself saying "I can't" try rewording it to "I don't *want* to." Then ask yourself if "I can't" has become an excuse for "I don't want to."

4. *Do I find that my mood is easily affected?* Moods sink with lack of sleep, poor diet, lack of exercise, or impending illness. Do you think your moodiness is related to one of these things? If so, it is easily remedied. Once you eliminate physical causes of moodiness, try to understand that moodiness may be a way of creating conditions under which you will or will not perform tasks. You use those conditions as an excuse for avoiding certain things. If that is true, then you need to understand what you are avoiding and, more importantly, why. Just as with procrastination, there may be a pattern to your avoidance, which you can identify and overcome.

87

5. *Is my work area cluttered and my time so fragmented that I am unable to complete tasks on time?* If your work area is a mess, it may be less a symptom of avoidance than a cause. If it is difficult to accomplish anything in the mess, you may give up. Clean it up. *Then* try working. You may actually enjoy the task now that it is not impeded by clutter. Often people who think, "I just don't have time for this now" really do not *make* time. Consider what you do make time for and what you do not make time for. Most of us make time for the things we want to do.

Learning from Others

The outcome of your interactions with others indicates whether you communicate effectively. If you find you are often unsuccessful—that you are not getting the desired outcome—you may find yourself sliding into a pattern of avoidance or forming a negative self-image. To learn from your interactions, ask yourself such questions as:

1. Why do people ask me to repeat what I say? Do I hold the phone correctly so my voice carries? Do I often eat, drink, or smoke while talking on the phone? Do I mumble or speak too softly?

2. Why do people ask me what I mean? Am I hesitant about stating the purpose for my call? Am I afraid to ask someone to do something for me? Do I understand the message or information I am calling to give?

3. Do people usually respond the way I expect? Do I fail to give people correct and complete information? By my attitude or what I say, do I encourage the person to respond a certain way?

88

4. Do I feel understood? Do I encourage the person to ask questions? Do I plan my call so that I make it clear who I am, what I do, and why I am calling?

5. Do I get the results I expect? Do I sound enthusiastic, positive, and self-confident? Is my request or instruction realistic and fair? Is my request or instruction directed to the right person to carry it out?

You can learn much about effective communication by observing others. Practice being aware of what they do that makes you feel that they understand what you say.

✓ Do they provide feedback by rephrasing what you say and repeating it back?

✓ Do they ask pertinent questions at appropriate times?

✓ Do they stick to the subject?

Try these techniques yourself when you communicate on the phone. Be aware of when your communication is successful and when it seems to falter. Think about the less effective conversations and how you would express yourself better next time.

Quiz Questions

1. The best way to deal with negative thoughts is to ignore them. Is this true or false? Explain your answer.

2. What is the key to maintaining professional objectivity?

3. Cite three steps to take charge of negative thoughts.

4. Give three examples, from the text, of positive language that can be used in place of negative language.

5. Define *self-fulfilling prophecy* and cite one example.

6. Negative attitudes can have less obvious, but nonetheless undesirable, results. Explain and give some examples.

7. One technique described in the text for maintaining a positive attitude is which of the following: suppressing negative thoughts, self-questions, self-fulfilling?

8. What is meant by "introspection?" How can it help you?

Discussion Questions

1. If you succeed in hiding your resentment from a rude caller, can you assume the matter is over when you have finished the call? Explain and discuss potential problems.

2. By looking honestly at your own attitudes, you can change negative ones. From the examples in the text, pick three sets of questions to ask yourself. Describe what positive answers to the first question in each set can mean.

3. Cite and discuss the solutions given in the text for overcoming three of the responses to each set of questions discussed in number two.

Activities

1. All of us procrastinate. Think of your procrastination pattern.
   Write down tasks you can think of that you have put off doing in the past month.
   Review your list.
   Look for similarities in the tasks. Have you avoided tasks that require you to use the library, or all assignments for a particular course? Put an A next to all tasks of one type, B another type and so on.
   Try to identify the causes of avoidance.
   Do you avoid using the library because you do not feel confident about finding what you seek?
   Do you feel uncomfortable in courses in which you have to use math?
   Write a plan of action to overcome your obstacles.

2. Practice converting negative phrases to positive ones or giving neutral phrases a positive twist. Think of negative things you commonly say or hear. If you cannot think of many right now, keep a piece of paper and a pencil handy to record ones you hear. When you have 10 or more negative samples, reword them to give each a positive tone. Try to be aware of negative things you say. Develop positive ways of saying them—without being untruthful or gushing. The next time you find yourself in a negative conversation be ready to turn it into a positive one.

Chapter Eight

Managing Stressful Calls

Upon completing this chapter you will be able to:

① *recognize four sources of stress in telephone work,*

② *recognize how stress affects your professional telephone skills,*

③ *reduce stress in telephone situations.*

Sometimes the mere ringing of a telephone creates stress. Most people are conditioned to respond immediately to the phone's bell. Whatever they were doing, they stop, wondering, "Who's calling?" "What is it?" Making calls can also be stressful; the caller wonders who, if anyone, will answer, and how that person will respond.

In addition, some kinds of work are highly pressured both on the phone and off. Deadlines and emergencies take their toll. And, when you sit and work for long periods, your muscles become stiff and tense.

Feeling stressed makes it difficult to project a positive image and to maintain your professional telephone skills. Even if you manage to continue behaving professionally and positively, by the end of the day you are tired, your head hurts and your muscles ache. If that continues over a long period of time, you risk burnout in your work.

Stress is never completely avoidable. However, it is not all bad. When stress is not overwhelming, it can be productive. It can heighten your anticipation, focus your attention, help you think quickly, and sharpen your performance.

In this chapter, you will see how stress occurs with telephone work and how it affects your professional telephone skills. You will also learn skills for dealing with difficult calls and relaxation techniques that you can practice at work or at home to help you manage stress.

Recognizing Sources of Telephone Stress

Attitudes toward the phone, the reason for a call, the nature of a job and physical conditions all contribute to possible stress in the use of the telephone—and all can be dealt with.

Attitudes Toward the Phone

Even the expectation of a pleasant call can cause the heart to beat faster, and receiving calls at certain times can elicit concern and alarm. Perhaps that morning call is from your boss, or that late-night ring is from an ill relative. Some people grew up in families where the ringing of the phone meant the arrival of big—usually bad—news.

Even if you are not alarmed when the phone rings, you may be startled. Usually the phone rings when you do not expect it. You have no warning, you are doing something else, and the call may be an interruption. Yet you feel required to answer immediately. The small jolt you feel as you change from thinking about what you were doing to thinking about the call is mildly stressful; you have a moment of urgency even if it turns out to be a call you are delighted to receive.

When you are the caller, you have more control—yet even then, you have no way of knowing who—if anyone—will answer the phone, or what will transpire. It is natural to feel a small amount of stress as you dial and wait for the response, even if it is so small that you do not notice it consciously.

Understanding why you feel stressed and taking steps described in this chapter will help you to deal calmly and professionally with each call that you make or receive.

Difficult Calls

In any job, some calls will be stressful. Common cases include callers who have complaints, are upset, or ask questions you cannot answer. Some calls are necessarily stressful, such as calls for emergency aid.

Yet, with any stressful call, how you perceive it and respond to it can make it more stressful or less. You might become upset yourself, consider complaints groundless, feel frustrated by unfamiliar questions, or panic when you learn of the emergency. Or, you can calm the caller, deal sympathetically with complaints, find out answers to questions, speed emergency aid on its way. Techniques described in this chapter will help you to remain calm, get needed information, and take appropriate action.

Difficult Work

Some jobs not only require a lot of telephone work, they also present many opportunities for difficulty and confrontation. Examples include:

✓ handling customer service calls for almost any business

✓ telemarketing, especially making outbound calls

✓ telephone bill collection

✓ medical, fire, or other emergency dispatch units

✓ switchboards in busy organizations or businesses

93

✓ businesses that have many urgent deadlines to meet, such as newspapers and advertising.

In jobs like these, workers need to recognize that stress is simply part of the territory.

Businesses or organizations where the pace is normally calm sometimes have occasions—such as a special sale or other event—in which telephone work is more stressful than usual. Employees will cope better if they understand that the situation is temporary and if they have given some thought to stress prevention.

Physical Causes

94

Sitting for hours in one position produces muscular tension. Keyboard workers, for instance, can experience headaches, backaches, and tiredness. You have probably experienced stiffness after remaining in one position for a long time—and know how good it feels to get up and stretch. When muscles are not moved, they become shorter and tighter; they need loosening and stretching. This chapter includes exercises to help you avoid painful muscular tension on the job.

Recognizing the Effects of Stress

Even though you recognize the presence of stress in telephone work, you may not realize how much it affects your professional telephone skills, your general on-the-job performance, and your overall health.

On Professional Telephone Skills

Stress will undermine your professional telephone skills. When you are stressed, you find it difficult to be courteous and positive. And, because stress is so distracting, it will make it hard for you to be a good listener—a serious concern, because listening is so important.

Stress also changes your voice. When you are stressed, you may speak too loudly or too softly, too rapidly or too slowly. Your pitch may rise and your tone will not be pleasant.

On Overall Performance

Stress affects not only your telephone skills but your overall job performance. It can even lead to burn-out. If working on the telephone is an important part of your job, you will not be able to minimize your exposure to it in order to relieve the strain.

You may have to identify the aspects of your job which are causing the most trouble. Be frank with your supervisor, ask for advice, and request additional training if you feel that would help.

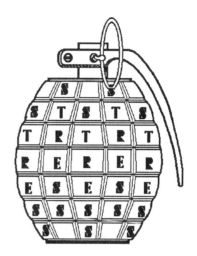

On General Health

It is a good idea to deal with stress *before* it deals with you. Over time, stress can have adverse effects on your physical health. Besides short-term muscular tension, which creates headaches and backaches, stress affects respiration and heart

Stress can create explosions of destructive energy unless you take positive steps to reduce it.

rates. It can lead to heart disease, ulcers, and digestive difficulties; aggravate other diseases; and lower immunity to sickness. If you are chronically stressed, you are less likely to take care of yourself. You may not eat carefully, may take too much alcohol to relax or smoke more. You may feel too exhausted at the end of the day to exercise properly, which could help reduce your stress. The less you exercise, the more tense you become.

Although stress is bound to accompany some telephone use, you can keep it under control and perform effectively.

Developing Skills for Managing Stress

Specific techniques help you deal with routine telephone stress, with particularly stressful calls, and with the physical causes of stress.

Routine Stress

When the telephone rings and you feel your heart rate pick up a little:

✓ Do not reach instinctively for the phone— prepare yourself. Take a breath, hold it a few seconds, then answer. You will hear what your caller has to say more clearly.

✓ Avoid answering the phone when you are in mid-conversation. Again, prepare yourself for the call. If you have to answer it, but are talking with someone else, finish your sentence, excuse yourself, then answer. Do not pick up the phone while you are still speaking. That is rude to the person before you and confusing to the caller. It is also stressful to you, because you are doing too many things at once.

Use active listening skills to prevent stress. Active listening, you recall, involves repeating the caller's message to make sure that you understand it, and asking nonjudgmental, fact-finding questions.

For example, you might receive a complaint from a customer about a fabric, advertised as stain resistant, which now has a stain. As the customer describes the challenge, you could ask "What did you do to it?" or you could ask "Do you remember what it was that made the stain?" The first question is judgmental and will make the customer defensive. The second is a nonjudgmental fact-finding question. When you ask nonjudgmental questions to find out exactly what is wrong and what callers want done, you diffuse the potential for stress and let them feel that they are getting the attention they need.

You will also be better able to keep your courage and your composure when you remember that complaints about your company's products or services are not attacks on you. Do not take them personally. You can sympathize with the customer, but you need not apologize unless you or the company is actually at fault. Stay calm and open.

Physical Stress

Muscles that remain in one position for a long time become tense. If your job is sedentary, you can take common-sense steps and practice the relaxation techniques described in this chapter. These activities will reduce muscular tension and help you to feel more comfortable.

1. *Make sure your work station fits you.* You may develop muscle tension if your chair is too high for the desk. Adjust your workstation so you can sit up straight with your head at a comfortable angle.

2. *Watch the caffeine and sugar.* Depending on your metabolism, you may find you have to limit your intake to avoid stress-producing coffee jitters and sugar highs.

3. *Move around, change positions from time to time.* If you have been sitting, stand up to take a call.

4. *Exercise every day.* Try to get some form of exercise daily, either in the course of regular activities or in a spe-

In the following conversation, the company representative uses active listening techniques to respond to a complaint from a customer, and to defuse the caller's initial anger.

Cust: I want to talk to someone who can get my money back to me.

Rep: This is Joe Brown, I'm the service representative, and I'd be happy to help you. Could you please tell me who is calling?

Cust: This is George Blodgett and I have been buying stuff from your company for years. But I've had it.

Rep: Thank you for doing business with us, Mr. Blodgett. We certainly want to resolve this situation to your satisfaction, so could you tell me about it and I'll jot it down to make certain I'm clear on all the details?

Cust: I put in an order for a case of your automotive adhesive four weeks ago and I told them I needed it really soon. And I sent a check. But I have waited and waited, and nothing.

Rep: I see. Do you happen to know the date of your order?

Cust: I don't remember. Don't you people keep records?

Rep: I understand your frustration, Mr. Blodgett. Do you have your customer service number there or a purchase order number so I can check it for you?

Cust: Oh, here it is...purchase order number 4040-7196.

Rep: Thank you, that's a great help. Let's see, your order of April 23 for one case of Double Duty Automotive Cement. That was two weeks ago. And you have not received it yet?

Cust: Oh, two weeks. Well, no, but I really could use it, I've got several orders waiting on it.

Rep: I'd be happy to put a rush on this for you. Would that be okay?

Cust: Yes, thanks, I really appreciate that.

97

cial exercise program. Walk or bicycle to work, to do errands, to visit friends. Park at the end of the parking lot or down the block and take stairs, not elevators.

Developing Relaxation Skills

Regular exercise relieves muscular tension that develops during the work day. But you do not need to wait for a lunch break or confine helpful exercises to before and after work. You can practice relaxation techniques throughout your workday.

98

At-Desk Exercise

These exercises can be done at your desk. They are ideal for those times when you need to move around but cannot leave your workstation. When you do the exercises, sit with your feet flat on the floor, tighten each group of muscles in turn, hold for a count of 10, relax.

1. Start with one foot, pointing your toes upward, then downward. Tighten and release your calf muscles, then your thigh muscles. Then switch to the other leg.

2. Tighten and release the muscles of your abdomen.

3. For each arm, make a fist, hold it, relax it. Spread your fingers. Flex your wrist, one way then the other. Pull your arm in, then extend it, relaxing in between.

4. Hunch your shoulders, then drop them. Stretch them as far back as you can, then bring them forward. Raise one shoulder, hold it, and drop it. Do the other shoulder.

5. To relax neck and head muscles, try these techniques:

    ✓ Turn your head gently all the way to the right, hold it, come back to center, then to the left.

    ✓ Gently drop your head forward and roll it gently from side to side; repeat four or five times.

    ✓ Raise your eyebrows as high as you can, hold, then lower them; repeat two or three times.

Visualizations

A *visualization for relaxation* is a series of steps that lets you relax and picture yourself in a peaceful, pleasant spot. A visualization can be as refreshing as a catnap. It will give all your muscles a change of position and provide you with a few moments of peace and quiet. A relaxation visualization only takes about three minutes.

1. Sit in a comfortable chair with your hands resting on your lap and your feet flat on the floor. Close your eyes.

2. Gradually relax every muscle, starting with those of your feet and legs. Relax the muscles of your thighs and hips, your hands and arms, your back, shoulders, and neck. Relax your face muscles; let your jaw drop.

3. Breathe deeply and for a moment allow yourself to be absolutely still and think of nothing.

4. Now picture some place you like to be, perhaps a favorite outdoor spot, a place you have visited. Visualize yourself in that spot, taking in the scene. Let yourself visit there a few moments, then picture yourself leaving.

5. Give yourself a minute to come back to awareness. Sit up straight and breathe normally.

99

Quiz Questions

1. Stress is totally negative. Do you agree? Why or why not?

2. What are some types of stress-producing telephone calls?

3. Give two examples of work in which telephone calls can be especially stress-producing.

4. How does stress affect professional telephone skills?

5. Cite two techniques that help in dealing with routine telephone stress.

6. Name two steps in active listening that help in dealing with angry callers.

7. Why does a person having a quiet desk job need to know about coping with physical stress?

Discussion Questions

1. Discuss how the telephone can create stress for both the caller and the person being called.

2. You have seen how stress can affect your professional telephone skills. Discuss the other effects it can have.

3. Discuss methods of reducing physical causes of stress mentioned in the text, and also methods that you have found to be successful in your own experiences.

100

Activities

1. Practice active listening skills in order to deal with stressful telephone conversations. Find a partner from your class for this exercise. Each of you should prepare a scenario in which you are the caller with a complaint. Briefly write out your imagined situation, which you can develop from real experience—your own or someone else's. Taking turns, call your partner up and role-play the complainer while the other person takes the part of the active listener. The two of you can agree on a time to do this, or you can agree to surprise the other person. To be as realistic as you can be, do not give the other person an unduly hard time; instead use your judgment to decide when to be responsive to and cooperative with the active listening.

2. During the next week make a point of noticing how and when you feel muscular tension; try taking steps to reduce the tension. Keep a diary for a week of your observations and note what you do about it. For example, you might note that after two hours of study in the library, you develop sore neck muscles. Try to observe whether the difficulty came from the length of time you were sitting still or from the height of the table or chair. Did you get up and walk around? Or do some relaxation exercises at your desk? The next time you were in the library did you take a stretch break after thirty minutes? Did that help? Or did you change to a different table and chair? At the end of the week, review your diary, and make a list of suggestions to yourself for preventing this form of stress.

Chapter Nine

Telephone Mastery Performance Appraisal Form

Here is a checklist of tasks and skills that you should be able to perform upon completion of this course. The numbers in parentheses after each item refer to the chapter that contains most of the material relating to that specific task. The tasks and skills are grouped into areas of general functions.

As you move through the course, check yourself and your performance against this list. Make copies to keep near you until you have checked off all the items. Do not check off an item until you find you perform the task or skill routinely, or that the condition implied is the norm for you. For example, you learn that an uncluttered desk with essential tools ready at hand is a standard of telephone mastery. If you tidy up your desk for one day, but let it become cluttered on the other working days, you should not check off the Yes column for the item regarding having an organized desk.

Do not check these items off until you have satisfied yourself that your desk and available tools, as well as your actions and overall performance meet the standard regularly over a period of at least a month. Try to check yourself against this list immediately after completing a call. Items marked with a telephone are particularly important.

One way to use this checklist is to make a copy for each week. During the week, check the Yes and No columns as appropriate. You will probably not have occasion in any given week to use all the skills. Check the chapters for those skills you marked No to reinforce or improve that skill. Save your old list and make a new one for the new week. This way you can evaluate your progress and pinpoint areas to work on. Use a highlighter to emphasize areas needing practice. Reward yourself with stars or other symbols rather than checkmarks for skills you have mastered.

Critical	Telephone Mastery Performance Criteria	Yes	No
	Skills For Call Preparation		
ℭ	Organized desk efficiently and neatly; had phone accessible. (2)		
ℭ	Tools always ready—message pad, note paper, pens, pencils, any special tools job requires. (2)		
	Had calendar visible; kept daily "to-do" list to remember important tasks. (2)		
	Kept a list of frequently called numbers organized for easy use. (2)		
ℭ	Used up-to-date phone book. (2)		
	Knew general features of phone book. (2)		
	Used phone book instead of calling directory assistance to save money. (2)		
	Skills For All Calls		
ℭ	Identified myself and company immediately. (3)		
ℭ	Made notes on file-sized paper, not scraps that can be easily lost. (2)		
ℭ	Was sensitive to other person's wishes to end conversations. (3)		
ℭ	Used interest comments to let speaker know I was listening. (4)		
ℭ	Used questions to clarify and provide feedback. (4)		
ℭ	Summarized and reviewed to be sure main points were covered. (4)		
	Used abbreviations to speed up notetaking. (4)		
	Identified potential listening roadblocks and worked to eliminate them. (4)		
	Used gestures, such as smiling, nodding, and shaking head, to be an active listener. (4)		
	Used notetaking and listening skills to learn about company and product. (6)		
	Asked questions of other employees to learn about company and product. (6)		
	Identified other sources of information about company and product. (6)		

103

104

Critical	Telephone Mastery Performance Criteria	Yes	No
	Skills For Outbound Calls		
	Prepared for outbound calls: verified name, number, and purpose of call. (3)		
	Obtained all information relevant to outbound calls ahead of time. (3)		
	Used knowledge of company and product to plan calls. (6)		
	Prepared a checklist and used it while making a call, especially a long-distance call. (6)		
ℂ	Was aware of difference in time in different time zones when making long-distance calls. (3)		
	Dialed direct whenever possible. (2)		
	Took advantage of toll-free "800" numbers. (2)		
ℂ	Allowed phone to ring 5-8 times before hanging up. (3)		
ℂ	Identified the purpose of the call after identifying myself and company. (3)		
	Rescheduled calls if contact time was inconvenient. (3)		
ℂ	Was not overly familiar with person called. (3)		
	Used voice mail technology effectively; spoke clearly and provided a complete message. (3)		
ℂ	Ended calls gracefully. (3)		
	Took advantage of answering machines by leaving clear and complete messages on them. (3)		
	Skills For Inbound Calls		
	Kept adequate supply of "while you were out" message pads. (2)		
ℂ	Had company directory with extension numbers readily available. (2)		
ℂ	Answered phone promptly—within two or three rings. (3)		
ℂ	Placed callers on hold only with permission; otherwise, asked them to return the call. (3)		

Critical	Telephone Mastery Performance Criteria	Yes	No
	Monitored the time caller on hold and every 30 seconds gave update, asking if caller wants to continue waiting. (3)		
	If not prepared for call, politely asked caller to hold while I obtained necessary materials. (3)		
ℂ	Transferred long-distance calls only with caller's permission. (3)		
	Recorded caller's full name, company, phone number, and complete message. (3)		
	Left messages where people could spot them easily. (2)		
ℂ	Waited for other person to hang up. (3)		
ℂ	Wrote down phonetically the spelling of names of callers I was not sure how to pronounce. (3)		
ℂ	Took notes for records and to help callers. (4)		
	Answered all calls in a positive, can-do manner. (3)		
	Exercised tact in telling a caller that someone was not available. (3)		
	Recognized the question behind the question that callers asked. (4)		
	Delivery, Fluency		
	Used the dictionary to find correct pronunciations of unfamiliar words. (5)		
ℂ	Paid attention to my speech and used good articulation. (5)		
ℂ	Used tone of voice to convey interest and concern for other person's needs. (5)		
	Adjusted the rate and volume of my speech to appropriate levels. (5)		
	Used exercises, posture, and breathing techniques to improve my voice. (5)		
	Stayed close to the natural pitch of my voice during phone conversations. (5)		
	Slowed my rate of speech when talking with someone who was upset. (5)		

105

Critical	Telephone Mastery Performance Criteria	Yes	No
	Used inflection and pauses to add emphasis to what I said. (5)		
✆	Spoke naturally and used spontaneous dialog (to avoid sounding like I was reading a script). (6)		
	Attitude		
	Was aware of negative thoughts so as to convert them to positive. (7)		
✆	Maintained a positive tone of voice. (5)		
	Used assertiveness and positive language to defuse other people's negative attitude. (7)		
	Identified signs of negative attitude and worked to overcome it. (7)		
	Used feedback from others to find areas for self-improvement. (7)		
	Used techniques, such as taking a breath before each call, to reduce stress. (8)		
✆	Reduced physical stress after sitting in one position a long time by moving around. (8)		
✆	Did some exercise daily, such as walking. (8)		
	Used five at-desk exercises to relax. (8)		
	Avoided stress-producing substances—caffeine, sugar, alcohol, nicotine, and such. (8)		
	Made every effort to do task at hand rather than put it off. (7)		
	Accepted questions and problems as challenges and opportunities. (7)		
	Was willing to try new, challenging assignments. (7)		

Glossary

Access Number: Number (often 9) dialed to reach (access) an outside line from a company phone. Some access numbers are restricted to local lines to prevent employees from making long distance calls. (3)

Active Listening: Listening that involves responding and encouraging the other person to speak. (4)

Area Code: Three-digit code assigned to a state or region, for dialing that region from another. (2)

Articulation: Producing the sounds of a word clearly, distinctly and smoothly. Also sometimes called *enunciation*. Compare *pronunciation*. (5)

Assertive: Firm, fair, and friendly. The most positive approach to getting what you need and want, as opposed to being easily put off or overly pushy. (7)

Automatic redial: Feature which allows phone to be programmed to remember a number and set to dial it continuously until the call is completed. (2)

Call Directories: Phones with the capability of taking calls for many other phones. Also known as *switchboards*.(2)

Company Policies: Rules that govern how business is conducted in a company, whether for making payments, offering warrantees, or answering the telephone. (6)

Computerized Touch-tone Phones: *Touch-tone phones* connected to computer programs that allow the user to do such things as record, screen, date, and relay messages. A user can also get a voice recording of tips or help by pushing one of the buttons, usually the # button. (2)

Conference Call: Call that makes it possible for three or more people in different places to take part in the same call. Offices may be equipped with phones that can handle conference calls;

otherwise, they can be arranged by an operator. Also known as *teleconferencing*. (3)

Consonants: All the letters of the alphabet that are not *vowels*. (5)

Direct Calls: Calls you complete yourself. Compare *operator assisted calls*. (3)

Directory Assistance: Service that helps you get numbers not listed in the book you have at hand. Commonly called *information*. (2)

Emphasis: Importance or weight given to words by pausing and raising or lowering *pitch* or *volume*. (5)

Enunciation: See *articulation*. (5)

Esophagus: the food pipe that leads to the stomach. (5)

Exchange Numbers: First three digits of a seven-digit phone number (not including *area code*). Exchange numbers identify a specific geographic area—towns or neighborhoods. (2)

Extension: One of several phones that can be reached through a single main number by dialing an additional *extension number*. A single desk phone may control more than one extension, in which case it will have buttons for each number which flash when that number rings. (2)

Extension Number: Additional number—usually three digits, but it can be two or four—for individual phones within a company. See *extension*. (2)

Feedback: Response of the person listening, which can include a direct spoken reply, as well as other clues, verbal or visual. (4)

Function Words: Prepositions, articles, and auxiliary verbs (be, do, have). Frequently eliminated from writing in the *telegraphic style*. (4)

Headsets: Combined receiver and microphone in a unit worn on the head or under the chin. leaving the hands free for other tasks. (2)

Hearing: Reception of sounds—the physical act of sound waves entering the ear and brain. Compare *listening*. (4)

Hold Button: Button on an *extension* phone that allows the person answering a call to put it on hold if another call comes in on another extension. (2)

Inflection: Raising or lowering the pitch of your voice. (5)

Information: See *directory assistance*.

International Access Code: Code used to dial a foreign country directly, without operator assistance. (3)

Introspection: Looking inside yourself, thinking about how you approach your life and work, and asking yourself questions. (7)

108

Larynx: The human voice box, located at the top of the *trachea*, where the *vocal cords* are located. (5)

Listening: Interpreting and understanding the sounds that enter your ear. Compare *hearing*. (4)

Local Area: The telephone area in which you need dial only the local number, not the *area code* or the numeral 1. (2)

Manufacturing: One of three major categories of business. Manufacturing companies are those that produce products for sale to other companies. For example, steel manufacturers produce steel for the automotive industry to use in making cars. Compare *trades* and *professional practices*. (6)

Matrix: Distinct situation or background of retained images—sights, smells, flavors—against which your memory is placed. (4)

Memory: Feature of a *programmable phone* that allows the phone to store phone numbers and dial them at the push of a button. (2)

Menus: Lists of which buttons on a *computerized Touch-tone phone* to push for different activities. (2)

Monotone: A voice with no *inflection*, speaking at the same, unvaried level. A voice that uses just one note. (5)

Operator Assisted Calls: Calls requiring you to dial the operator to make the call. These include collect, person-to-person, bill to third party, mobile land, air and marine, conference, and international calls. (3)

Organization Chart: Chart that shows how a company is organized into various groups by function. It also indicates a written or unwritten order of decision making, reporting, communication, and specialization of activity. (6)

Pharynx: Passageway at the top of the throat through which both air and food pass on their way to the lungs and the stomach. Connects to the *trachea* and the *esophagus*. (5)

Phone Book: See *telephone directory*. (2)

Phonetic Spelling: Writing the word as it sounds to you without worrying about the correct spelling. (4)

Phonetically: How something sounds. For example, if you were to spell the word "phone" phonetically, it would be *fon*. (3)

Pitch: How high or low, as in music, a voice is. To some extent determined by age or gender; also by smoking, stress, and other controllable factors. Compare *volume*. (5)

Policies: See *company policies*.

Professional Practices: One of three major categories of business. Includes law, medicine, and engineering. Many employees in these professions have advanced degrees. Compare *trades* and *manufacturing*. (6)

Programmable Phone: Phone with frequently dialed numbers stored in its *memory*. (2)

Pronunciation: Voicing the standard, accepted sounds in each word. Compare *articulation*. (5)

Push Button Phone: See *Touch-tone phone*. (2)

Rate of Speech: How quickly you speak. (5)

Retention: Capacity to remember, including things you may not be conscious of having retained. (4)

Rotary Dial Phone: Phone with a circular disk with holes in it. Each hole opens on a number from 0 to 9 and a set of three letters. When you dial a number, the disk makes an clicking sound as it moves back to its starting position. (2)

Rote: As if reciting from memory. (6)

Screen: To sort out one kind of call from another; for example, if your supervisor wishes to speak only to certain individuals, your job would be to *screen* out all others. (3)

Self-fulfilling Prophecy: An expectation that comes true because you expect it to come true and act in a way to bring it about. (7)

Shoulder Rests: Attachments enabling you to tuck the receiver between shoulder and ear, leaving hands free. Shoulder and neck muscles can become cramped using them. (2)

Speaker Phone: A phone with a microphone capable of picking up voices at a distance and a speaker that can broadcast loudly enough to be heard by a room full of people. Makes it possible for several people to participate in a telephone conversation. (2)

Switchboards: Machine capable of handling calls for many phones. A *call directory* is a small switchboard. (2)

Tactile: What is felt. One type of information (the other is *visual*) that is not available to people talking on the phone. (1)

Telegraphic Style: Style used writing headlines, which entails eliminating *function words* and other secondary words wherever possible. (4)

Telemarketing: The use of the telephone to generate revenue by making sales, handling orders, providing customer service, or arranging appointments for selling. (1)

Teleconferencing: See *conference call*.

Telephone Dialog: Prepared material, including opening remarks, a description of products or services, a benefit statement, and fact-finding questions, used in presenting a product for sale over the telephone. (6)

Telephone Directory: Alphabetical listing of people's and businesses' names and phone numbers. The *phone book*. (2)

Time Zones: Regions into which the country and the entire world are divided, in which the time changes one hour as you move from zone to zone. Eastern zones are earlier than western ones. There are four time zones in the continental United States: Eastern, Central, Mountain, and Pacific. (3)

111

Tone of Voice: Emotional quality of your voice. (5)

Touch-tone Phone: Phone with four rows of three buttons each, representing the numbers 0-9 and the symbols # and *. They make different toned beeps in the receiver for each number pressed, hence the name "Touch-tone." Also called *push button phone*. (2)

Trachea: Air pipe leading to the lungs. (5)

Trades: One of three major categories of business. Includes businesses such as construction, lawn care, electrical work. Many employees in these businesses are trained in technical skills, such as plumbing, tree surgery, electrical wiring, and may be licensed or certified by a government agency or trade association. Compare *professional practices* and *manufacturing*. (6)

Transfer: Switching a call from the central phone to an extension. (2)

Visual: What is seen. One type of information (the other is *tactile*) that is not available to people talking on the phone. (1)

Vocal Cords: Folds of tissue that close the *larynx. (5)*

Vocal Expression: The sound of your voice, influenced by five factors: *tone, pitch, rate of speech, volume,* and *emphasis*. (5)

Volume: Loudness or softness of your voice. Compare *pitch*. (6)

Vowels: The letters *a, e, i, o,* and *u*. (All other letters of the alphabet are *consonants*. (5)

White Pages: Pages of the *telephone directory* containing general information and the alphabetical lists of names and numbers. Compare *yellow pages*. (2)

Yellow Pages: Section of the *telephone directory* with advertisements and listings for businesses and services. Compare *white pages*. (2)

Index